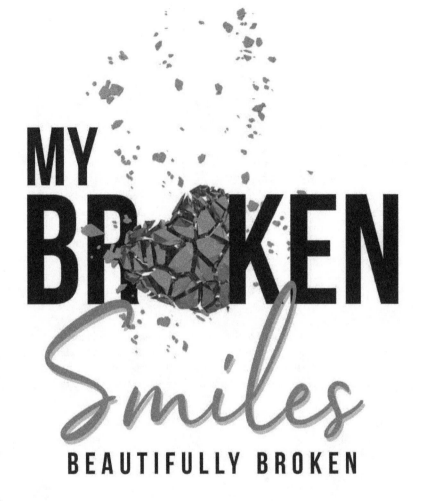

MY BR KEN
Smiles
BEAUTIFULLY BROKEN

MELANIE SMILES

MINDFUL MISSIONS
Oak Park, MI

MY BROKEN SMILES: BEAUTIFULLY BROKEN
© July 2020 Melanie Smiles

ISBN-13: 978-0-578-71735-7

Mindful Missions
Oak Park, MI

Printed in the United States of America
First Edition August 2020

Design: Make Your Mark Publishing Solutions
Editing: Make Your Mark Publishing Solutions

contents

foreword

First, I would like to say that I am truly honored to be considered to write a foreword for Melanie Smiles. Melanie and I attended the same high school, Oak Park High School in Oak Park, MI. At that time, I did not know Melanie because I was two grades higher than her, but I am so excited that I know her now. Mel, as I call her, is a very genuine, loving, and honest person. I have been able to grow closer to her as her faith coach. Mel has blossomed beautifully, and she is not afraid of her past or anyone trying to stop her future. I admire her for breaking barriers and telling her story without apology, so she can help others. As I read her story, tears rolled down my face, knowing how hard it must be for her to tell her truth. I urge everyone who has been rejected or felt insecure to read this amazing book. I am genuinely excited about her future. Melanie is very transparent in her story of triumph so other women can grow, and for that, I salute her.

Minister Laticia Nicole Beatty

introduction

*T*his book is about my personal experience with brokenness and transformation to emotional healing through the word of God, family, mentors, faith, and prayer when I surrendered it all to the Lord. I will share with you real events; life-changing circumstances; my experience with pain, brokenness, abuse, marriage, divorce, and unforgiveness; and how I made it through and became the person I am today.

This book will take you on a journey through the many events that happened in my life, mainly in my marriage, that contributed to my brokenness and how I learned why God allows us to be broken. Throughout the chapters, you will see how the enemy uses people and their brokenness to break other people and gain access into people's lives. I will share how to recognize and identify some of the causes, traits, consequences, and bad fruit of broken individuals.

By sharing my story of God's wonderful works in my life, I hope to encourage and educate others facing the same or similar issues and inspire them to seek and know the same God that saved and changed me.

No one escapes life without seasons of hurt, suffering, darkness, trials, storms, affliction, or brokenness. In those seasons, it doesn't mean God doesn't love you or has forgotten about you. We view hurt, trauma, suffering, and brokenness as thieves because they rob you of your joy, peace, energy, ability to love, self-worth, and trust. But God meets us right there in our pain, lifting us up, protecting us, and guiding us toward something new as long as we allow him. We can become better when we can identify our brokenness and the source of it, embrace it, and seek help.

I'm here to let you know you are an overcomer, and you can overcome brokenness and all power of the enemy. My prayer is that the words of this book will encourage, inspire, or aid you in healing. You can let go and remove yourself from a place of brokenness and not carry it around from relationship to relationship, from season to season. You can move from unforgiveness to forgiveness by following God's plan for your life. Beauty is not in brokenness itself, but in how we allow it to transform us into better versions of ourselves.

chapter one

SPIRITUAL BROKENNESS

Before God saved me, I was spiritually broken, and my brokenness was a doorway for the adversary to present himself as an angel of light and a Godsend, masking his demons and brokenness. "Broken" is a separation or something not working properly—something that is interrupted, damaged, shattered, needs repairing, not whole, or wounded. Brokenness interrupts our lives and separates us from anything that keeps us from living our best life, leaving a person feeling unhappy, hopeless, incomplete, discouraged, depressed, or wounded.

Satan uses brokenness as a window of opportunity to enter our lives, causing negative thoughts and more pain. In our brokenness, people can attach their negative spirits to our lives in a way that can ultimately destroy us. Satan and his demons are spirits that search for humans to use. Satan is smart and charming. He knows God's word and knows how to present things to us to gain access to us. Therefore, he won't appear as a violent, evil-looking devil dressed in a red suit with horns and a pitchfork. He can take on many forms and can, very well, be disguised today as a beautiful angel of light. Satan is a powerful spiritual force, but he is not as powerful as God.

As long as we are here on earth, at some point we all will be approached by the enemy and his schemes. We will be tempted, afflicted, and tried by him. We are in constant war with the enemy and our minds. The enemy wants nothing more than to gain access to our hearts and minds. There is a lot of truth in the old saying, "An idle mind is the devil's playground." Our life is shaped by our minds. If Satan accesses our mind, he can influence our thoughts. Our thoughts shape our decisions, our decisions shape our actions, and our actions are what we do. The battle for sin always starts in the mind. King Solomon said it best, and this is why God's word tells us,

> "*Above all else, guard your heart, for everything you do flows from it.*"
>
> (PROVERBS 4:23 NIV)

The Word also tells us,

> "*For as he thinks in his heart, so is he.*"
>
> (PROVERBS 23:7 NKJV)

The enemy looks for ways to access us through our brokenness, insecurities, loneliness, childhood pain, failures, abuse, shame, losses, relationships, our past, environment, and vulnerabilities, including but not limited to drugs and alcohol. This is why drugs and alcohol are so powerful and have such a strong hold on people, especially our children.

Drugs and alcohol cause us to lose the ability to think and act rationally, leaving us unguarded and vulnerable. Drugs and alcohol give the enemy easy access to us, which leads to addiction, loss of control, strongholds, unhealthy behavior patterns, brokenness, soul-ties and sex-ties, spiritual depression, negative spirits, and mental and physical illness.

My spiritual depression was the root cause of a lot of my struggles, low points, bad choices, feelings of incompleteness, and unfulfilled needs. A need or unfulfilled need can become dangerous because it creates a place of vulnerability within us. I am a giver and very empathetic; I enjoy helping and serving others. Being spiritually depressed and an empath, I attracted some negative and narcissistic spirits into my life.

Empaths are givers and highly sensitive individuals who tend to put other people's needs, feelings, and desires ahead of their own. They absorb other people's emotions and feelings as their own, sometimes taking on the pain of others at their own expense.

Narcissists are attracted to empaths; they become the perfect predator and feed off of them. A narcissist is someone with a personality disorder that is self-centered, lacks empathy, has a sense of entitlement, and has a deep need for attention and admiration. Narcissists are takers and put their needs ahead of everyone else's. They take and drain until there is nothing left to take. This is why their victims are left feeling drained and depleted.

Narcissism, or narcissistic personality disorder (NPD), is a mental illness. Narcissists are broken individuals who experience a deeper connection of something happening spiritually, emotionally, and psychologically. We hear a lot of people being called narcissists these days; narcissism appears to be more prevalent in our society. It does have a broad meaning, and there are different levels of narcissism, which can be confusing because it mimics other traits and can be hard to identify or understand.

According to research, other victims of NPD, and my personal experience, sociopaths and malignant people with NPD demonstrate some strong traits and characteristics. Some of the more consistent traits are that they lack empathy and respect for other people and their feelings. Narcissists are pathological liars, masters of disguise, and manipulators. They create trauma bonds and relationship entanglements. Initially, they are the most charming, affectionate, humorous, godly, and nicest people we might ever meet. Then they show their true selves as mean and heartless.

Dr. Patrick Carnes, founder of the International Institute for Trauma & Addiction Professionals and author of *The Betrayal Bond*, developed the term "trauma bonding." By his definition, trauma bonding is the misuse of fear, excitement, sexual feelings, and sexual physiology to entangle another person. Trauma bonds are similar to Stockholm syndrome and occur when we go through periods of intense love and excitement with a person, followed by periods of abuse, neglect, and mistreatment.

Narcissists' actions don't reflect their words. They will confess their love early on and may try to convince you of being their soulmate. They are hypersexual, showing sexual promiscuity and reckless behavior. Because they are bored easily, narcissists have a number of short-term marriages or relationships. They often have unexplained time loss or will disappear for days, weeks, and months with no notice or closure, leaving you feeling worried, confused, drained, and hurt. They gaslight you, which is a form of psychological manipulation and emotional abuse. Gaslighting is a hallmark of narcissism. Their gaslighting can have you doubting yourself or things you know to be true and questioning your own sanity. They often get sympathy with terrifying stories about their past relationships as if they were abused or victimized. Narcissists can be flashy and appear to be responsible and have it all together, but they are immature, irresponsible, and don't take responsibility or ownership of their actions. They mismanage time and have no respect for others' time or appointments. Narcissists play victim, lead double lives, and will chronically lie as a way to maintain power and control over their victim's reality.

Narcissists are wolves in sheep's clothing, but they can also be pillars in the community, like preachers and ministers of a church. They mask who they are and have two sides or two faces. The face they show to the world is the charming, confident role model—the godly side. The other side they hide from the world is dark and deceitful—their true nature. They act out this nature by deceiving people with their positive, counterfeit side. These characteristics are usually pathological and consistent in people with NPD.

In a relationship with a narcissist, you might constantly find yourself explaining the basic elements of human respect to a full-grown adult—things that neurotypical people would understand, like the fundamental concepts of honesty, respect, and kindness. Many people suffer true pain and devastation at the hands of sociopaths, malignant narcissists, or loved ones with NPD. Victims of these individuals often leave with post-traumatic stress disorder and other debilitating brokenness.

chapter two

SOMETHING ABOUT ME

I grew up in a two-parent Christian household and was raised by a God-fearing, praying, loving, and supportive family. I was raised in church and baptized at an early age. I knew God, but I didn't have a consistent relationship with him. Although I had a praying family and was taught to pray about everything, my prayer life wasn't that strong. Most of the time, I waited until bedtime to pray my traditional prayers of "Now I lay me down to sleep," or "The Lord's Prayer," along with any prayer requests. I occasionally read the Bible and memorized some scriptures, but I didn't know the importance of it.

If I'm honest, I really didn't know how to use the Bible. I didn't understand what I was reading at times or know how to apply it to my life. I didn't know the Bible could answer my questions and help me navigate and thrive in life. I didn't know it could teach me how to hear God's voice, break generational curses, heal, give me peace, and make me whole. I didn't know what putting on the full armor of God was, and I didn't know the full armor could protect me and my family from the enemy.

At age fourteen, while visiting a friend's church, I had a special encounter with the Holy Spirit that confirmed his presence and made me believe God is real. Yet, throughout the years, I wrestled between God's way or my way, and most of the time my way won. My way led me to become a teenage mother of not one, but two kids, before graduating high school, along with a multitude of hard struggles.

Being a high school student with two kids from two different fathers was painful. I heard just about every negative, shameful, degrading, and hurtful name about me that you could think of. I could hear the judging and see the disgrace on people's faces when they saw me: this little, five-foot, one-hundred-and-five-pound teenager carrying an infant and pregnant with another one. Some of my friends' parents didn't want them hanging around me anymore, feeling I was a bad influence. They said I wasn't going anywhere in life and I had thrown my future away. Hearing those things hurt; I was ashamed, embarrassed, and wanted to crawl in a hole and hide from the world. Not to mention how badly I hurt and disappointed my parents ... I didn't have a clue how I was going to climb out the hole I had dug for myself. I just knew I couldn't stay in that pit.

For those who judged me, nailed me to the cross, and

counted me out, I wanted to prove them wrong. I started using those negative comments people were speaking over my life as motivation. I was determined to be triumphant to cover up the shame and guilt of being a teenage mother. I didn't like depending on others or asking for help. I hurt my parents and lost their trust; therefore, I didn't want to be a burden to them. I worked, found a townhouse twenty miles away from my parents, moved out, and was able to graduate high school on time. After high school, I worked full-time, including every weekend and most holidays.

I utilized the welfare system, educational grant funding, and any low-income opportunity I qualified for to help me reach my goals. I didn't abuse public assistance; I used it for a short time to establish a better future for my kids and me. I worked full-time, went to college, accomplished several certifications, and earned a license in cosmetology. I worked two jobs and went back to school for several years until I graduated nursing school and became a registered nurse. All this persevering and accomplishing goals didn't leave much time for God.

Throughout the years, I carried this unexplained void and feeling of emptiness. No matter what I accomplished, how great my relationships were going, or how much I was loved, that unexplained emptiness stuck with me. I always felt better when I prayed, went to church, listened to gospel music, or helped others. I also felt better being in a place of praise, worship, and the presence of the Lord, but those feelings were only short-lived.

Unlike most young girls, I never had dreams of getting

married or desired a fairytale wedding because I never thought I could love anyone enough, or for long enough, to marry them. In most of my relationships, the romantic love seemed to prematurely die out, which structured the thought that I was incapable of loving someone enough to marry them. Small things like the way they chewed their food, acted too clingy, couldn't fix a flat tire, didn't go to church, didn't have relationship with their kids, acted too fearful, or couldn't do simple home repairs were turn-offs for me.

I came from a big family of long-term marriages, including my parents' and grandparents'. To me, they appeared to have healthy and beautiful marriages. I loved how they loved and cared for one another. The husband took on the role as head of household, taking the lead. The husbands in my family were hardworking; they provided for, protected, and took very good care of their wives and kids until the Lord called them home.

I saw my grandmother and mom as virtuous women. God-fearing, praying women, lacking nothing of value, they were loving, hardworking, giving, respectful, attentive to their husbands' and families' needs, and wise counsel. They were also some of the best cooks in town, who kept the house clean and trusted the leadership of their spouses. I loved their love and desired to love and be a great wife just like them. For me, to be able to give that kind of love, I needed to love someone enough to give it.

It wasn't that all the men I dated were bad or losers. Most of them were pretty good, hardworking men who loved me, and I loved them. Yet, the relationships weren't strong enough to endure. I realized I was comparing the qualities and standards of men I dated to those of my dad and granddad. If the men were lacking in any area of values, morals, or significant qualities my dad possessed, the relationship wouldn't go far.

After my best friend, Sala, was murdered by her husband, the incomplete feeling and fear of falling in love grew stronger. I remember having a conversation with my friend Teresa years before, thinking something might be wrong on the inside of me because I fell out of love so easily. I didn't want to settle or marry someone just because he was a good man or financially secure. I have a lot of love to give and wanted to give it happily and freely. One time, I was engaged, and the thought of planning a wedding placed a gnawing, dull pain in my upper stomach combined with a feeling of nausea. I remember thinking, *Nope. I can't do it.*

I wanted to marry someone I could love hard and give my best to, someone who knew God's word, prayed, and went to church. I wanted someone my children could talk to, respect, and learn from—a provider, a leader, and a handyman who loved to travel. I felt like I was looking for a knight in shining armor who really didn't exist, so marriage wasn't on my heart at all. That all changed when I met this beautiful smile that changed my life forever.

chapter three

A BEAUTIFUL SMILE

Another busy twelve-hour work shift down, and I was ready to go home. I was a registered nurse working in the emergency department of a busy inner-city hospital in Detroit. I approached the time clock too early to clock out, yet too exhausted to wait the few extra minutes. I swiped out and left. I got in my truck, rolled down the windows, opened the sunroof to catch a breeze, and enjoyed the little sunshine that was still present.

Halfway home, approaching a red light along side of me, a very attractive man on a three-wheel motorcycle with his music playing pulled up. He turned my way and said hello with this beautiful smile. Eagerly waiting to get home, shower, and get off my feet, I waved, said hi, and looked back toward the light. He honked his little horn and said,

"Call me," yelling out his cell number twice and his name: Myls. He winked at me and drove off as the light turned green. I dismissed the encounter and continued my drive home.

It wasn't until about the second day or third day after the encounter that I thought again about that wink and beautiful smile. With the way my memory is set up, only by the grace of God would I be able to remember his number. As I thought about the numbers he had yelled out, I began to write down what I thought he had said. Several days later, I decided to try calling the number. No one answered the number I called, but a voicemail greeting said, "Thank you for calling Myls Home Improvement. Please leave a message." I couldn't believe I had remembered the number!

I left a message and waited for Myls to call back. He didn't call back. A few days went by, and I decided to try calling again. No answer. I didn't leave a message that time and made up my mind that I wasn't calling again. About five minutes after I hung up, my phone rang, and it was him.

Hello?" I answered.

"Good morning. How are you?" he replied.

"I'm good. You?" I asked.

"I'm blessed," he responded.

"Do you know who this is?" I asked.

"Yes," he said. "I've been waiting on you to call."

"I called and left you a message," I reminded him.

"I am so sorry. I've been so busy working midnight shifts, taking care of my kids, and running my businesses. I haven't had time to call anyone back, but I have been thinking about you every day. Please forgive me. Can we start all over? Hi. My name is Myls. What's yours?"

I knew his clever excuse felt shallow, but I proceeded to introduce myself. We had a lengthy conversation during which he shared lots of information about himself, past relationships, and his assets and businesses, which were many. He had a good sense of humor and spoke with great intelligence. He also appeared to have a keen interest in my life and asked many questions. He was definitely a long-winded talker. He admitted he could talk about anything with someone who was a good listener, and he did. I was impressed with his wisdom, knowledge of the Lord, and his success. He spoke highly of his children and how actively involved he was in their lives. He said he was a loyal, loving man who had never been in love before and was looking to love the right woman.

Myls told me he worked the midnight shift at an automotive plant and had his own contracting and home repair company. He was also a real estate investor, a minister, and the owner of multiple businesses. I asked him why a man of God with good character, values, and success was still single. Myls said he had been married once before and hadn't found that special someone. He revealed that over the years, he had received about ten engagement rings from different women. I mentioned that concerned me and laughed. He believed women knew when they had a good man. He said it wasn't that they weren't good women, just not who he wanted to marry.

As we were approaching the end of the call, Myls asked if

we could pray. He had mentioned early on in our conversation that he ministered at a small church in Detroit and invited me to visit one day. I was impressed, as I had never had anyone I just met pray with me. He took the lead in the prayer, quoting scriptures to support his knowledge of the Bible and leaving a lasting impression. Myls said he really enjoyed talking to me and was in need of someone to talk to.

After we prayed, Myls said, "I heard the Lord say, 'Be careful how you handle and treat her, for she is fragile yet gentle. She will love you more than anything, but her mouth is her best defense and weapon.'"

"The Lord just told you that?" I asked.

"Yes. I'm gonna let you go, but I need to see you sooner than later," he said, ending the call.

A couple weeks went by and we met for our first date at Diablos Cantina, a restaurant he chose for dinner and salsa dancing. Myls was such a gentleman. He was charming and he serenaded me. His compliments were followed by recited poems and riddles that fit the topics of our conversations. Myls spoke on the importance of and the need for having what he called "the three C's" in his relationship: communication, consistency, and compromise. He also told me he didn't drink or smoke and reminded me that he was a loyal and faithful man looking for the same in return.

Myls asked lots of questions as if he wanted to know all about me that night. He wanted to know the things that turned me on and off, with specifics. He asked my favorite color, artist, songs, movies, concerts, and foods. He even asked how I behave when I'm upset or respond in anger, and he wanted real-life examples. In my mind, I wondered about his method of getting to know me. I was okay with Myls asking questions, but didn't he know he would have to discover some of these things on his own? A person can tell you anything, but it might not align with their actions and character. I told him how important trust and honesty were for me, and how a relationship couldn't thrive without it.

Myls looked me in my eyes and assured me, "That is very important for me as well. Melanie, I would never do anything to jeopardize our trust, nor do I have any intentions of hurting you."

The atmosphere was perfect, and the food was delicious. He suggested I order extra for lunch the next day at work, which I thought was a kind and thoughtful gesture. After dinner, we went salsa dancing. We walked down Maine Street, talked, and laughed for hours. He was so attentive and protective of me.

"Are you always this attentive and affectionate?" I asked.

He handed me a beautiful rose from a man selling them and said, "Not with everyone. Everyone doesn't deserve it. I have never met a woman like you before. You're special, and God told me to make you my study. Let's plan a trip to Mackinaw Island, the Poconos, or anywhere you like."

"Whoa! Let's slow down!" I replied. "This is our first date. I don't know you like that to be going out of town with you. We are just getting to know each other. Let's first get to know one another before we start making moves like that."

"What else do you need to know?" he asked. "I'll tell you whatever you want to know. Just ask."

I laughed. "It don't work like that for me. People will say anything to get what they want. I need to learn you for myself and see your actions," I said.

"How long will that take?" he asked.

"I don't know. It depends on what you show me," I said.

"Well, take your time, but hurry up," he warned jokingly. When I laughed again, he took my hand, looking very serious. "I'm serious, Mel. God already told me you're the woman for me."

"Okay," I replied, feeling doubtful. I looked at my phone and noticed it was after one in the morning. This seemed like the perfect time to end the evening.

Over the next few weeks and months, I was showered with "Good morning, beautiful" texts, calls from Myls, morning prayers, calls just to see if I needed anything, flowers, and food delivered to my job. He hand-wrote love letters, gave me gifts, and took me to the movies, ice cream socials, blues in the park, and bike nights. We were having a good time getting to know one another. Although I was enjoying Myls and having the time of my life, I was feeling the effects of late nights out and long and exhausting work shifts. Myls was the ultimate charmer and knew all the right things to say and do, which made me endure some nights of getting only three hours of sleep for a busy twelve-hour shift.

We would go to the mall, and if there was an outfit or perfume Myls liked or wanted me to wear, he would ask me to try it on. If he liked it, he bought it. He would tell me how amazing I looked and would encourage me to wear the outfit home right then. That was a turn on for me, and

I wanted to do all I could to make him smile. In pure bliss and excitement, I showed off all my gifts, clothes, food, cash, and other things Myls bought me to my family and friends.

I remember bringing home a beautiful coat and a candle set Myls had bought and saying to my daughter, "Myls is the kind of man you want in your life—someone that will spoil you, love on you, and treat you like a queen."

Her response was, "That man must really love you, Ma. He's always buying and doing something nice for you."

To show my appreciation and gratitude to Myls, I wanted to reciprocate the kindness. I cooked his favorite dishes, arranged special dates for us, and bought him nice things. He was impressed with my cooking and how I centered him and incorporated something he liked into our dates. I wanted him to receive full enjoyment of the occasions I planned for him. I shared with him that I am a giver from the heart, a nurturer, and that I love to help people when I can. He said he could tell based on the way I loved on my family and others.

Myls confessed his love for me early on.

"How do you know you love me?" I probed. "You said you've never been in love before, so how do you know it's love this time?"

"It feels different, like no other, and this is what I've been praying for. The Lord confirmed that you're my soulmate," he assured me.

His words reminded me of an actor reciting lines from a stage play. I liked him but it had not manifested to love yet. When I tell someone I love them, it's genuine and from the heart. Each time we spoke after that, and each time we were together, Myls ended the call or said goodbye with, "I love you."

We were together almost every day I wasn't working, hardly leaving time for anything else. Days I would normally spend with family or on household chores, errands, or handling personal business matters were spent with Myls. Although I was enjoying the excitement of a new relationship, the attention, and being with someone I saw as my dream come true, I needed to catch up on reality. I was missing my family, and I was missing important calls from placing my phone on vibrate to avoid too many distractions from giving Myls my full attention. Myls had three cell phones that were silenced most of the time, and he hardly answered his phone no matter who was calling. That concerned me. I did check my phone occasionally and answered some calls in case there was an emergency with kids or family.

I remember asking Myls, "You're not concerned about your family calling or a family emergency?"

His response was, "No. If it's an emergency, they should call nine-one-one. That phone gives me anxiety. It's always somebody calling wanting or needing something. Every day I'm helping, giving, or doing something for someone else. I'm doing exactly what I want and I'm where I need to be. Whoever is calling will call back if it's important. When I'm with you, I'm at peace and nothing else matters. God has placed something special in my life, and I'm not letting anything or anyone come between that."

Things were going well months into what turned into a

faster-than-normal relationship for me. We began meeting one another's families. Upon meeting his family, I noticed I was the only one calling him Myls; they called him Tory. He said Myls was the name the streets gave him, and he didn't like everyone knowing his real name.

Over time, I noticed Myls was missing more of my calls, and the time he took to return my calls was getting longer. I didn't make it a big deal, given that he was such a hardworking, devoted man of God who worked nights, ran his businesses during the day, and still found time for me. I needed that time to catch up on rest, work, family, and other things, anyway.

Myls was aware of my work schedule and my responsibility as a nurse, but I noticed at times it seemed he didn't too much care whether I got any sleep for work. He would talk as if he was concerned and cared, but he would say something right after to make me feel guilty or change my mind.

For example, one time I had worked three twelve-hour shifts in a row in the ER, each day hanging out late with him after work. It was after midnight and I had to be at work at seven the following morning. Myls mentioned he wanted to take a ride on the motorcycle. My response was, "You go ahead and enjoy your ride; it's late and I have to be up early for work."

In his calm, soft-spoken tone, Myls replied, "Baby, I'm not going anywhere without you. I understand you need your rest. Those patients depend on you to take care of them. I need you to be rested so you can do your job safely.

"I only get a couple months out of the year to enjoy riding

my bike, and I look forward to riding any chance I get. We don't have many nice days left this season for me to ride. You are important, and we have to be willing to sacrifice some things for the ones we love. But I don't want to be the only one sacrificing, giving up everything and losing myself in the mist."

Hearing that, I was confused, wondering where that came from. It was the first time I had suggested Myls go anywhere without me or conveyed anything that went against pleasing him. Regardless of how I expressed understanding his enjoyment of riding his bike, and suggested he still take the ride without me to unwind, Myls refused to go, making me feel bad about my decision.

He began expressing how much he needed me and didn't want to have to go to any other woman, or person besides me, for anything. At this point, it was late and I was sleepy. My brain felt like I was drunk, and I was trying to stay awake and listen. Myls appeared upset that my face and body gestures mirrored my exhaustion while he was still talking. I'm assuming he felt as if what he was saying wasn't important to me.

He said, "If sharing my concerns with you is putting you to sleep, we can talk about this another time when you feel like listening. Get your beauty sleep, but save some sleep for the ugly people." For the sake of not endlessly going back and forth and staying up any longer, I went to sleep.

We entered a new season in our relationship. Myls and his family suffered devastating losses in their family, including the loss of his ex-wife, the mother of his two youngest sons.

My heart was hurting for Myls and his family, but more deeply for his sons, whom I had not yet met. It became even harder for me to reach Myls or get him to answer his phone. Sometimes an entire day or two would pass with no word or return call from Myls. I was concerned and worried, and wanted to make sure he was okay, or even alive. When I finally heard from him, he would say he was just going through a lot dealing with losing so many people in his life. I understood his pain and wanted to be there to support and comfort him during those times.

Around that time, Myls also received bad news that a family member down south passed away. Family members said they had been trying to reach Myls to inform him of his uncle's declining health. They were unable to reach him in time, and that sad news was a shock to Myls.

Seeing the man I was falling in love with grieve and mourn was heartbreaking. It was important to me that he knew how much I cared, empathized, and was there for him. I provided support, compassion, a listening ear, and sensitivity during this time. He expressed again that he needed me and that it was important for me to be by his side during these times. He asked me to accompany him to the funeral and spoke of me needing to meet the rest of his family.

One of the most important people there he wanted me to meet was his sister; he told me about their close relationship and his protective, brotherly love for her. Myls said his sister was a reflection of his mother, who was resting in heaven. He warned me that his sister was protective of him as well and might not be so friendly toward me when I met her.

Just days before leaving for the funeral, Myls purchased a Mercedes Benz and wanted to drive it down south to the funeral. Preparing to hit the road, we stopped to pick up his cousin to ride along with us. We took turns driving, and I was first to drive on our way to Alabama. Driving through Ohio, I got pulled over by the Ohio State Police for speeding. I handed the female officer my driver's license, and Myls handed her the vehicle registration and insurance. She asked me who the vehicle belonged to, and Myls said the car was in his sister's name. The officer asked me to step outside the car and escorted me to sit in her patrol car and wait for her.

She returned to the patrol car after a few minutes and asked me who Leah Forson was. I replied, "I don't know. I've never heard that name before."

The officer pushed, saying, "If Tory is your boyfriend, why don't you know the name of his sister or whose car you're driving?" My response was that he had several half-sisters I hadn't met, and I was sure Leah was one of them. She ran all our names through her data system, cleared us to go, and told me to slow down and drive safe. Feeling relieved about not getting a speeding citation, my spirit still desired to know who Leah Forson was. I asked Myls who Leah Forson was, and he said it was the person he bought the car from. He explained that he hadn't had a chance to transfer everything into his own name yet. He assured me, "If you want, we can put it in both our names. You know whatever I have is yours, baby."

When we arrived at our destination, Myls's family welcomed us and showed me plenty of love. I was flattered by how affectionate and protective Myls was. He spoke highly of me to his family and made sure I was comfortable and wanted for nothing. Initially, his sister seemed unapproachable, but she later unveiled her big heart, compassion, and love for her family.

Myls confessed his love for me to his family and told them he was going to marry me. The home-going celebration for his uncle was beautiful. With respect to the occasion, I was happy to meet and support Myls's family and share those moments with them.

chapter four

DATING A SMILE

*T*he time had come for me to celebrate another year of life with an intimate gathering of close friends and family at one of my favorite restaurants downtown. Myls informed me ahead of time he had to work the evening of my birthday dinner, and he probably wouldn't make it.

A couple hours prior to my birthday dinner, I was at home getting dressed when Myls called and confirmed he couldn't get off work. He was disappointed that he wasn't going to make my birthday dinner, and I was sad I wouldn't be sharing my birthday gathering with my man.

"I do have a little something for you," Myls said. "Open up the door." I opened the front door, and to my surprise Myls greeted me with a huge custom-made rose floral arrangement with my favorite colors, along with a beautiful card, gifts, perfume, a gorgeous watch, and cash.

He apologized again for having to work and said, "If you really want me to be there, I will call off work for you." I told Myls he should go to work and I thanked him for my birthday gifts and said there would be plenty more days for us to celebrate.

Things weren't getting any better with Myls answering his phone. Days later, I called him and he didn't answer. I couldn't understand why a man with three phones was so hard to reach. Considering he worked nights, I gave him time to sleep in before I called. Maybe lack of sleep had finally caught up with him, and he was sleeping in longer. I waited until evening to call again. This time, Myls answered.

"How is my PJ?" he chirped with the sounds of machinery and drills in the background.

"Hey!" I replied. "Who is PJ?"

"That's you!" Myls answered. "You are my PJ—my pride and joy." His answer was endearing and pleasing to hear, but it felt like false flattery. I told him how sweet it was to be considered his PJ, and I also asked if he had received any of my calls and texts.

"No, baby. I've been working on this roofing job all day." I thought he was home sleeping, so why hadn't I heard from him all day?

"Are you saying you worked all night and day without any sleep? Why couldn't you return any of my calls?" I asked.

Myls told me that after work, he had slept in the parking lot for about two hours before heading to the job site since he was behind on work and the homeowner was complaining. He said he never received any of my calls and he thought something was wrong with his phone. Myls then said he heard one of his uncles was in the hospital and he had been feeling a little sad thinking of him. I was about to say something else, but he cut me off quickly.

"I need a date with my soon-to-be wife. You know I miss you, right? It's time for us to start going to church together more often." Even though it was probably less than forty-eight hours since we had last seen each other, I felt he was trying to smooth things over to stop me from asking more questions.

I explained to Myls the importance of consistency and communication in a relationship just as he had mentioned early in our dating the importance of the three C's. The lack of communication, not answering his phone, and inconsistency were going to affect the growth of our relationship if they were not resolved. I told him I wasn't expecting him to answer my every call because I knew there were times when he couldn't answer right away. I understood that he worked, got busy, and couldn't take every call. But I also explained that to consistently go eight, nine, twelve hours, or even days not hearing from my man was not going to work for me or the relationship.

"I'm not sure if it's something personal you're dealing with, or if this is your normal way of doing things. Either way, it has to be fixed, because I don't see us getting very far like this," I explained. "Communication is important in building a healthy foundation in any relationship." Myls apologized once again and said he would do better. He also said he would give me a special ring tone so he would know it was me calling.

If Myls was working on one of his rental homes or a nearby contracting site, I often brought him lunch and checked to see if there was anything else he needed. I also prepared home-cooked meals for his lunch before he went to work. His plant job was almost forty-five minutes away, and Myls didn't want me driving that far to bring him lunch.

One day, I was preparing one of Myls's favorite meals and wanted to bring lunch to his job, but he insisted that I not bring it because of the driving distance. I told him I didn't mind since he often brought me lunch at work, often even surprising me with lunch. Doing that for Myls would be a pleasure, and I thought it was important that I know where his job was in case of an emergency.

Myls agreed, saying his woman should know where he works, especially in case of an emergency.

"Please don't think I don't want you to know where I work," he continued. "It's just you are a very caring person, and I've never had anyone really care that much about me to want to know. God forbid anything should happen; I want to be reachable. I need to be reachable for you. I will have my phone on, waiting for your call, even though we aren't supposed to have our phones in the plant. I'm doing this for you. Call me when you're on your way so I can give you directions and guide you in."

A couple hours later, I texted Myls letting him know I would be leaving shortly to head his way. The food was done;

it smelled good and was packed nicely in new Pyrex food containers I bought specifically for his lunch. I was excited and couldn't wait to get it to him so he could enjoy his lunch at work.

I called his phone just like he had asked, but the call went straight to voice mail. Thinking maybe someone else was trying to call at the same time I was, I called again. The call went straight to voice mail again. After about thirty minutes of trying to reach him, I headed back home and put the food in the refrigerator. He knew I was coming, so why didn't he answer? I couldn't believe this man had me do all that cooking and preparation and then did not answer the phone.

Hours after midnight, I was in bed asleep when I received a text from Myls saying his phone had died and he had left his charger at home. He said he would call me in the morning. I immediately tried calling him, just seconds after the text came through. His phone rang, but he didn't answer. There was no sense in trying to call back only to get sent to voice mail. Heavy emotions and unsettling feelings started boiling inside me. All kind of thoughts began to infiltrate my mind, which made me unable to go back to sleep.

The next day at work, I got a call, followed by a "Good morning, my PJ" text from Myls. I was still upset about the night before, so I let his calls go to voice mail and didn't respond to his text. Normally, when I was at work and unable to take his call, I would either call Myls back as soon as I could or send him a quick text acknowledging his call. The delay in getting back to Myls was anywhere from five minutes to an hour, depending on my work flow and patient care. He also had my work number in case he couldn't reach me on my cell or needed me urgently. That day, I didn't rush to get back to Myls.

When I was driving home after my work shift, Myls called. I decided to answer, pretty sure he was wondering why I hadn't responded. He asked if I was okay and wanted to know why I didn't return his call. I told him I was upset that he had me cook all that food for him and didn't answer my calls as I was en route to bring it to him. I told him I didn't play games and I was tired of having the same repetitive conversation and issue. I wasn't buying any more of his excuses about his disappearing acts, his dead phone batteries, the texts he never received, or the illnesses. He turned the conversation around on me.

"Are you saying you intentionally didn't answered my calls?" Myls raged. "What if I was in danger, needed you, or I was stranded on the side of a road? I would never intentionally ignore your calls. How can you get mad at me for not answering my phone because it died, and I work at a plant where no cell phones are allowed? You're sitting up here mad at me for not answering my phone, but you are doing the same thing to me!"

I reminded Myls this was the first time I had purposely not answered his calls and that there hadn't been an issue with me being unreachable. He tried to defuse the situation.

"Listen, I know I can be a handful sometimes and have narcissistic tendencies, but two wrongs don't make a right. We need to get an understanding so we won't keep hurting each other in the process. Baby, we can fix these issues;

nothing is too hard for God. Let's talk about this tonight over that dinner I was supposed to get yesterday. I'm sure it will be just as good today, if not better. I love to eat your food when you're happy and loving. Your food tastes better when it's made with love.

"When you want to fight with me," Myls continued, "think about what is good, what is right, what is pure, and lovely. Because I'm not eating anybody's food who is mad at me. You had a long day. I need to get you a key to this house so you can stop questioning and worrying about me. Go home, grab the food and your overnight bag, and come on over so I can rub those feet. You been up all night worried about me and working all day. I'm going to run your bath water, rub your feet, give you a full body massage, and make sure you get your rest."

That's exactly how the rest of the evening went.

chapter five

HE PROPOSED WITH A DIAMOND RING

Over the next month, I noticed Myls's efforts and improvement with communicating, being reachable, and following through on his word. We attended church together, and I was pleased at his effort to show how much he cared about my feelings and wanting to have a healthy, respectful relationship. It made me want to reciprocate every action but with double portions of love, respect, generosity, attention, and the most humbling acts a woman can pour into someone she's falling in love with.

Myls's birthday was approaching, and I wanted to do something special for him. What do you buy a man who has it all? Literally, he had over three hundred bottles of designer cologne, a massive luxury watch collection, tons of jewelry, more than fifteen cars, several trucks, three motorcycles, over a dozen homes, and enough designer suits, shoes, and clothes to fill a department store. I came up with the idea to create or plan something money couldn't buy.

I love planning and doing things that allow others to feel loved and appreciated. I receive joy any time I can assist in cultivating and harvesting the feelings of love, gratitude, and togetherness. I wanted to take Myls someplace he had never been but always wanted to go, somewhere intimate, romantic, exciting, and memorable that would leave a lasting impression. I did some research and found what I thought would be the perfect place to take him.

I didn't tell Myls where we were going, as I wanted it to be a surprise. He said he had always wanted to see and experience the fall leaf colors up north. As we drove into Traverse City, Myls was captivated by the fall scenery and was taking pictures, noticing small details of the surroundings, speaking on its beauty, and admiring how the changes in the season correspond to the seasons in our lives.

At our resort, we had a luxury two-room suite with a beautiful balcony beachfront view, a remote fire place lounge area, TVs visible behind light-mirrored walls of glass accenting the bathroom, and a Jacuzzi with a silver tray of chocolate-covered strawberries. Two champagne flutes and a bottle of champagne sat inside a shiny stainless steel bucket.

I had planned a horseback trail ride on a beautiful private ranch. Myls was a little nervous because he had never ridden a horse before. He was open to the experience, and in no time he saddled up and he and Winston, the horse, became friends. We had a great time horseback riding. Our weekend was full of going on adventures, sightseeing, conquering fears, trying new things, shopping, and fine dining of his favorites: prime rib and seafood.

Leaving Traverse City, we made it back home in time to go to the concert of one of Myls's favorite artists. It was his finale birthday gift. I got us front row seats to see recording artists Avant, Ginuwine, Tank and some other R&B stars. Myls was happy at the end of the night and said I had made him feel special. He said this was the best birthday gift experience he had ever had, expressing his gratitude and saturating me with affection. I was happy and full of joy, knowing I was able to put that smile on his face and leave an impression on his heart.

Sweetest Day weekend came around, and Myls got us tickets to see Ledisi in concert. Dressed and ready, I waited for Myls to pick me up. The doorbell rang, and I opened the door to an extremely handsome, charming, sexy Myls. He walked into my home smelling good and dressed to impress. He reached for my left hand, got down on one knee, looked into my eyes, and said in his sexy, smooth voice, "You know I love you, right? From the day we met, I knew you were someone special. God told me you were going to be my missing link, someone I can talk to and share my secrets with. I've been pregnant long enough, pregnant with a promise, and God said it's time to give birth to everything he promised me. Baby, I need you." Myls pulled out a little red box and opened it, revealing a beautiful shiny diamond ring that looked exactly like the ring I had tried on at a jewelry store and told him I liked.

In that blissful moment, my mouth dropped and tears filled my eyes. I was taken by surprise, full of emotions, and elated. He expressed his love for me, referring to me as a virtuous and noble woman. Then he said, "Melanie, will you marry me?"

I was still in shock, yet overjoyed with what just happened. It took a second for my lips to move. He said, "If you need to take some time to answer, take your time, but hurry up!"

In my Kelly Price voice: "He placed it on my finger, and I said *yes!*"

chapter six

ENGAGEMENT AND WEDDING PLANNING

*U*nlike most girls, I had never desired or envisioned myself having a wedding. I told Myls I didn't necessarily need to have a wedding if he didn't want one. I was just happy to be marrying someone I truly loved and who truly loved me and God. Myls said he wanted to have a wedding because this marriage meant something to him, explaining that with his first marriage, they only dated for three months and didn't have time for a wedding. Myls said most weddings were all about the bride, and her family usually took over, but not this one!

"This will be our wedding," Myls explained. "It won't be just about you or me, and I want to be involved in everything."

Most men wanted to be relieved of any wedding planning, if possible. I considered myself blessed to have a man who wanted to be involved and was just as excited as I was about the wedding.

The engagement was in full effect. We set a date and planned a wedding for the following year, in the spring. I was excited, and my love for Myls was growing and growing each day. I had never met such a loving, generous, praying, God-fearing man in my life. I remember thinking God really smiled on me when he sent this beautiful smile. Since I was about to marry my true love, I wanted to do everything right. I wanted to give my best, be a great wife, and please God.

Although Myls had gotten better with answering his phone and communicating with me, I noticed other small things that bothered me from time to time. He would often tell little lies about things he didn't have to lie about or have a different answer for certain things we had talked about before. He owned several professional musical instruments like guitars and keyboards, and he had told me how much he enjoyed playing all those instruments. One day, I asked him to play something for me since I had never heard him play any of the instruments. He replied, "I don't know how to play any of those instruments. I just like collecting things and thought and thought I could learn how to play from YouTube."

Another time, he told me he was sitting in the church parking lot about to walk into service and would call me once service was over. About ten minutes later, he butt-dialed me, and I overheard him talking to his cousin Marvell about painting and pest control for a vacant house they were working on. Later, he told me how much he had enjoyed the church service that I know he never went to. Even though his lying bothered me and made me become more aware of things, I mentally excused it. After all, I hadn't caught him doing anything wrong; he was actually working. He was probably behind on a work project and didn't want to hear my mouth about overworking himself and not getting any sleep.

Soon, the holidays were over and we entered a new year with our wedding plans going strong. I still hadn't met Myls's two youngest sons and was disappointed we didn't get to spend any time with them over the holidays. I often mentioned them to Myls. His response was that since their mom passed, they hadn't been responding to any of his calls or texts. He said it was something he needed to handle and that he would go by and check on them the following weekend. I had noticed Myls having increased anxiety and sensitivity when we spoke of the kids.

I never got a clear understanding about why the communication and visits with his sons suddenly stopped after the passing of their mom. Having such a devastating loss would impact their lives forever, and I felt they needed all the love, prayers, and support we could give them, especially from their dad. I understood the sensitive nature of them losing their mom and respected Myls's decision to address the concerns of his sons at his discretion. I wanted to know more, though, because my instincts were telling me there was more to the situation than what Myls was telling me.

The wedding planning was going along just fine until Myls started adding up the prices. He said he needed to set a budget because if he didn't, I would end up spending all our money on the wedding and we wouldn't have any left for our marriage. To avoid any problems, Myls set our wedding budget at eight thousand dollars, and I was not to surpass the set budget. By no means whatsoever was I happy with the budget he set. We were inviting one hundred and fifty people, plus our wedding party. I couldn't do it with just eight grand. He reminded me that it wasn't *my* wedding; it was *our* wedding.

"My sister only spent a few hundred dollars for her wedding, and it was nice," Myls told me. He smirked, saying, "It's going to have to work because that's all I'm going to spend on it, anyway."

I understood his logic and knew within my heart that spending less was the right thing to do. Marriage is about compromise and respecting the reasoning of your spouse, and I didn't want to go against what he said. I complied with our set budget.

From choosing our wedding party, colors, invitations, venue, and menu, Myls participated in every step. If there was anything he knew I really wanted for the wedding, he gave in and adjusted the budget to make me happy. Our family, friends, and wedding party were very supportive and generous. Our loved ones were excited about our union and wanted to contribute and bless us in any way they could.

The bridesmaids' dresses finally came in and it was time for the ladies to try them on and finalize their payments. A few loved ones from our wedding party came in from out of town to finalize their fittings and payments. Myls and I scheduled time to meet with them at the bridal shop. My future in-laws and I arrived just minutes before Myls did. Myls walked into the bridal shop with a young lady. He greeted me and the rest of the family with big hugs and apologized for the delay in getting there. Myls's family was excited to see the young lady.

He introduced me, saying, "Alaysia, this is Melanie. Melanie, this is Alaysia." I smiled and said hello. He told me her mother was at work and he had to pick her up from school.

I didn't want to make anyone feel uncomfortable so I waited until no one could hear me ask. "Who is Alaysia?" I whispered.

"My daughter," Myls replied. "Remember, I told you about her."

"Daughter?" I asked, confused.

"Yes, my daughter."

"Myls, I don't remember you mentioning you had a daughter. All this time, why haven't you brought her around or spoken of her like you speak of your sons?"

"Baby, I know I have. Maybe you forgot," Myls explained.

"That's not something I would forget," I insisted.

"So now what? You don't want to marry me because I have a daughter?"

"It has nothing to do with you having a daughter," I explained. "Your children are a part of you. If I love you and marry you, I will love them as well. The problem is I don't remember us talking about her. It put me in an uncomfortable situation. I'm hoping she doesn't feel like I'm acting funny toward her or intentionally left her out of the wedding. Are there any more kids or anything else I need to know about?" I asked.

"No," Myls replied. "But listen, Melanie. If you don't want to marry me because I have a daughter, or if you're not ready to get married, then say that and I will understand." I told him this had nothing to do with me not wanting to get married. It was about communication. I suggested we talk about it later since I didn't want anyone to hear what we were talking about, especially Alaysia.

The rest of the day, I felt a little sad and unsettled. I wondered if I had been so caught up in the wedding planning that I hadn't remembered Myls's daughter. I wondered if he purposely never told me he had a daughter. I tried to recall him ever mentioning anything about her, wondering where she had been all this time and why I was just meeting her. I started thinking of times he might have mentioned her. Myls went to work that evening, and we didn't get a chance to talk about it.

Myls was big on date nights. After a night out at the movies, we went back to my house and talked about our wedding song choices. He had a couple songs he wanted me to hear that he said reminded him of his love for me. The first song he played was "Love Was Made for Us" by Cleo. I had never heard of the song or the artist, but it was the most beautiful song I had ever heard. It captured my heart instantly and painted a genuine description of my love for

Myls. The next song was "I Found Love (Cindy's Song)" by BeBe & CeCe Winans. Myls said he chose that song because he finally found love when he found me. Feeling my emotions, listening to the songs, listening to Myls, and thinking about how much I loved him made my eyes swell with tears.

"Doll, I didn't mean to hurt you, and I apologize for not communicating with you the way I should have about Alaysia. It's a long story why I wasn't able to bring her around all this time, and I will tell you all about it. Just not tonight," Myls explained. "She is my daughter, and I love her."

"I apologize if you told me and I didn't remember. If she is a part of you, then I want to be a part of her life as well," I said.

Myls wiped the tears that had trickled down my cheek. "God knows how much you mean to me," Myls said. "I'm going to make sure I get this right. He said it's very important that we go to church together and stay rooted in the Word. So when the enemy comes, which he will, especially after we get married, he won't be able to destroy what God has joined together. The devil is mad because he knows God is about to do something powerful with this marriage and in our lives."

That night we read scriptures from the Bible, prayed, talked about what we received from the Word, and talked about our upcoming marriage counseling sessions with my pastor, Bishop Ellis of Greater Grace Temple. I woke up the next morning to another beautiful love letter from Myls, conveying his love and the unlimited possibilities of where our love could take us if we trusted God. He also brought me lunch at work, along with a beautiful bouquet of roses accented with our wedding colors and a card expressing his love.

chapter seven

BRIDAL SHOWER & RESURRECTION DAY

few weeks before our wedding, I was preparing for my bridal shower. After multiple attempts to call Myls, he texted me to tell me this was a rough time of year for him as he mourned the loss of his beloved mother resting in heaven. He said he needed some time to himself. My heart dropped, and I shared his feelings of sadness and grief. I wanted to show Myls my love, attention, and support. I wanted to comfort him, console him, listen to him, and be there with him and for him. I told Myls how much I loved him, and I reminded him that he didn't have to go through this alone. I couldn't focus on the wedding at all because my thoughts and concerns were with Myls and making sure he was okay.

A couple days went by, and no one had seen or heard from Myls. He wasn't answering his phone. I went by his house a couple of times, and he wasn't there either. I became worried and anxious, praying he was all right. For the first time, I called the number he had given me for his job at the auto plant. It was a general public number, and the operator said she didn't know why he would have given me that number.

I thought of my close family friend named Lynn who worked at the same plant as Myls and called her to see if she could help me find him. She contacted the night shift supervisor to ask about Myls, and the supervisor told Lynn no one with that name worked there, in any department. All kinds of thoughts started running through my mind.

Late in the midnight hour, I reflected on something I remembered Lynn had said something a couple months back about the plant having a two-week shutdown over the holidays. Myls had never mentioned a shutdown and didn't take any days off work. At that moment, I got on my knees and started praying. I couldn't rest or sleep the entire night.

The next day, Myls finally called, apologizing for not answering my calls. He said he had gone into a period of sadness, reflecting on all the people he had lost. I told Myls it was okay to grieve, but it was never okay to isolate himself for days in that emotional mindset, especially without letting someone know where he was and whether he was safe. I also told Myls how worried and concerned I was about him, reminding him that this was not an appropriate, respectable, or safe way to handle that or treat me. "When you hurt, I hurt," I explained. I wanted Myls to understand how important it was for us to figure out how to handle stress and grief together as a married couple.

Thoughts were still festering of Myls not being an employee at the plant. I explained I had something important I needed to talk to him about and that I would be over after work.

Later that evening, I met Myls at his house and once again mentioned how important honesty and trust are to me. I was concerned that we might need to reconsider getting married if we were having another breach of trust. He asked what the problem was and why was I saying those things.

I asked, "Why did you give me the wrong number to your job? I was told you didn't work there, and there is no one by your name working there. During the holidays, the plant was shut down for two weeks and you lied about going to work. So tell me—what's really going on, and where do you go at night?"

Myls's face and eyes took on a look of evil. His eyes, red from lack of sleep, made him look even more upset. Myls initially tried to keep up the lie until I proved him wrong again and he became more upset. He started accusing me of being loud and confrontational.

In anger, Myls said, "Yes! I did lie about working midnights at the plant. I lied because I thought you would like or respect me more if I worked a nine-to-five job or punched a clock." My facial expression must have ticked him off more.

"Most women don't respect my business as a real job. I don't always feel like being bothered with people or want to be found. I like to have my space and be alone some nights without being obligated to something or someone," Myls continued.

"You didn't think about that before you asked me to marry you?" I demanded. "How long did you think that would work once we got married and moved in together?"

"I don't know, and I've been thinking about that."

The more I tried to explain the importance of truth and honesty or mentioned other questionable things, the more upset Myls became. I finally told him I was uncomfortable going into marriage with these issues.

"Melanie, since you can't trust me and I'm such a horrible person for making one small mistake, how about we call off the wedding, and you can leave! Since you're so perfect and never make any mistakes, you don't need to marry a human being like me that makes mistakes," Myls challenged.

"Myls, I never said you were a horrible person. We all make mistakes. I'm not being confrontational or yelling. It seems like you're making up things to say about me because you're upset about getting caught in a lie. Do you mean what you said about calling off the wedding?"

"Yes," Myls declared. "The wedding is off. Melanie, you got the answer you came here looking for. You can go now."

I couldn't believe this was happening a week before my bridal shower! I got into my truck and cried. I was confused and hurt, and I felt like I was living a bad nightmare. I needed someone to talk to. Still sitting in his driveway, I called Myls's sister to let her know what happened and tell her Myls had called off the wedding. She was in disbelief as well and suggested I pray about it in hopes things would work themselves out. I was embarrassed to call or tell anyone else at the time.

It had been a couple days since Myls had called off the wedding, and I had yet to hear from him. The wedding was less than a few weeks away and all plans, preparations, and last-minute to-do lists were paralyzed. The bridal shower was in a matter of days, and no one, not even the rest of the bridal party, knew our wedding had been called off. Since I had not spoken to Myls, I wasn't sure whether he had told anyone.

I wasn't even sure if Myls was serious about calling off the wedding. I thought maybe he had just been upset and had said something he didn't mean. Either way, the silence, hurt, isolation, and stress were weighing on me. Thinking of all the planning, hard work, and money our loved ones had put in for our wedding, and having to notify them within only two weeks of the cancellation of the wedding, was extremely painful and was eating me alive.

Easter weekend arrived and the day of my bridal shower. My bridesmaids planned my bridal shower at an undisclosed location. When I arrived, guests were already there. The room was sparkly and beautifully decorated. My sister, Kim, prepared an elegant menu around my favorite foods. A massage therapist was there, offering massages for the ladies throughout the day. I appreciated the love, support, gifts, creativity, and the precious time my bridesmaids, family, and friends poured into giving me a lovely bridal shower.

They minimized my stressors and any involvement

in the planning by simply requesting my presence at the shower. Everything was amazing, and I couldn't have asked for anything better other than to actually have a wedding. The traumatic and emotional pain of being celebrated as a bride-to-be for a wedding no one knew was called off was unbearable. I masked my pain with a smile, and I never mustered up the strength to tell anyone.

After the bridal shower, I drove my bridesmaid, Tequia, to her car that she had left at another bridesmaid's house. In the car with Tequia, I couldn't hold it in any longer. I needed someone I trusted to talk to. She was shocked and surprised about the wedding being called off, but she wasn't surprised about the other things I told her. She'd had some personal concerns about Myls that she had held back for the sake of my feelings and happiness. She said he came off as too good to be true, and she had sensed that his behavior was not genuine, as if he was hiding something. She never wanted to say anything to me about it because Myls made me happy, and she didn't have any facts to back up her concerns. She apologized for sharing her thoughts and didn't want her opinion about Myls to weigh in on any of my decisions.

The day after my bridal shower was Easter Sunday. I went to church alone, and I still hadn't heard from Myls. I didn't attempt to call him because I wasn't the one who had called the wedding off. I was waiting for him to contact me and handle the situation like an adult. I wondered if he enjoyed making me feel miserable or if it was his way of having power over me and the situation. I couldn't understand how someone could act like this right before their wedding and make a major life decision in the midst of emotional exhaustion. I understood that as human beings, we get upset and sometimes say or do things we don't mean. But after we calm down and think things over, people usually reconnect, apologize, and talk about it—especially if they are truly sympathetic or apologetic about their actions.

It had been almost a week since I had heard from Myls. He knew about all the work, people, and money that had gone into planning the wedding, and he knew whether he wanted to get married ... or not. I was starting to think maybe he didn't regret saying what he had said. Maybe Myls had been having second thoughts about getting married, and this was his way out. If that was the case, we needed to deal with it and get closure on it as soon as possible. It wasn't fair to all the people who put their time, money, and work into making sure we had a nice wedding.

Late on Easter Sunday, fear of the unknown, mental unrest, and the drawn out silence won their battle with me. I decided to be the bigger person and call Myls. To my surprise, he said he was waiting for me to calm down and call since I was the one who was upset and didn't want to get married after I found out he lied about not working at the plant. He said he had wanted to call me but couldn't handle anymore rejection from me. He apologized again about lying to me and wanted to right his wrongs.

"I didn't say I didn't want to get married," I reminded Myls. "You called off the wedding."

"Baby, I said a lot of things I didn't mean that night because I was hurt and disappointed in myself for lying to you about something I didn't have to lie about. I had a lot to think about this past week, and I couldn't stomach the thought of losing you. I have lost enough people in my life, and I'm not about to lose you over something like this. There's something about you, Melanie, that's different. You're special—unlike any other woman I've been with.

"I've been in counseling with the pastor, I confessed my sins, and I'm studying Bible scriptures that are working in me. From this day forward, Melanie, I'm going to tell you the truth and be transparent about everything. Make sure you can handle my truths, because everybody says they want the truth until they don't like what they hear. Everybody can't handle the truth because sometimes the truth hurts. I'm considerate of your feelings and careful about what I say to you because truth without love is still brutality."

Myls asked me not to abuse him with the truth, even if it meant lying to him to protect his feelings. He went on to say he could lie, say, or do whatever he wanted to other women without caring about their feelings.

"But *your* feelings matter, Melanie," Myls explained. "God's really been talking to me this past week, and he showed me there's only so much he's gonna allow me to do to his daughter." I listened to everything he said and shared my thoughts.

"As far as truth goes," I explained, "there is a way to convey truth without brutality. It's okay to be considerate and sensitive of other people's feelings, and as long as the truth is given with kindness and respect, you're not responsible for how someone reacts. At this point, there shouldn't be anything we can't talk about to one another. I don't want a marriage built on lies and trust issues."

"I understand, and I want to give you everything you need as your husband. In return, I need you to give me everything I need as my wife," Myls offered.

"Wife? Didn't you call off the wedding?"

"No, I didn't," Myls said.

"Well, that's what you told me."

"I was so upset that night, and I don't remember saying that. I'm so sorry. I do want to marry you, and I hope you still want to marry me," he said.

"You really don't remember saying the wedding was off?" I asked skeptically.

He sighed, as if he didn't want to go back and forth about this. "Melanie, I know I said some things that night to hurt you, and I promise I will spend the rest of my life trying to make it up to you if that's what it takes. This past week, I was miserable without you. God has been working with me, and I'm letting you know I want us to get married. I need you. I want you as my wife for life."

After hearing all Myls had to say, I told him I loved him, explained how much he meant to me, and talked about how much I valued marriage and wanted to be the best wife I could be. I also told him his needs were important to me, and I wanted to give him everything he needed from his wife.

"I still want to marry you, too," I told him. Our wedding plans were resurrected on Resurrection Sunday.

chapter eight

THE REVELATION

For the weekend of our wedding, family and friends arrived from different states to witness our marriage vows and join us in celebrating. Things were coming along as planned—no stress, no anxiety, and no bridezilla moments. I was excited and looking forward to being Myls's wife. Although my bridesmaids wanted to plan a bachelorette party, and I appreciated their kind thoughts for wanting to do so, I respectfully declined to have one. My maid of honor, bridesmaids, family, and sister, had been such a blessing throughout the wedding planning, making things almost easy for me. Instead of a bachelorette party, I wanted to spend a peaceful day and evening before our wedding at home, preparing and praying.

The night before the wedding, as I was at home preparing

and enjoying talking, laughing, and reminiscing with my guests, I received a call from Myls's family asking if I had seen or heard from him. I hadn't heard from him since earlier in the day. They asked me to call him since they had been calling and trying to reach him all day. They were expecting to gather or have some sort of bachelor celebration for Myls, but they'd been unable to reach him. I tried calling him to let him know they were looking for him, but he didn't answer my call, either.

One of my bridesmaids, a friend of over twenty-five years named Rachel, had flown in with her family and stayed at my house for the wedding. Later that evening, as Rachel and I sat on my bedroom floor talking and reminiscing, my phone rang. It was Myls. I told him his family had called looking for him, and the groomsmen wanted to celebrate with him tonight. He said he was finishing up last-minute work when they called and he knew what they were calling about. He said he would return their call but didn't want to hang out or celebrate that night. He wanted his alone time with God that evening. I told him to finish getting settled in and I would call him later to finish talking and to pray with him before we went to bed.

Overhearing our conversation, Rachel laughed and asked whether the groomsmen were partying without the groom. We both laughed.

"Chil' ... that man is something else, but I love him."

While Rachel and I were talking, I noticed she became quieter. I invited her to share what she was thinking.

"Do you really want to know how I feel?" Rachel asked doubtfully.

"Yes," I said.

"Are you sure you want to know?" I wondered why she was asking like this. All of a sudden, Rachel teared up and started crying. I was at a loss for words and couldn't understand what was happening or why she was crying. Did she know something about Myls that I didn't? I thought she liked him. When we visited her in Atlanta last year, I thought we all had a good time together.

"What's wrong, Rachel?" I asked. "Why are you crying?" Rachel looked me in my eyes.

"Mel, he is not who you think he is," Rachel revealed. "He is going to hurt you."

"What are you talking about? Do you know something or have you heard something about him?" I was getting nervous.

"I am so sorry for bringing this up the night before your wedding, but I've been having these disturbing thoughts and revelations for some time. I didn't want to tell you because I didn't know how you would take it, and I didn't want you to be mad at me."

"Where are these thoughts coming from?" I asked.

"I don't know, but from time to time, I receive revelations about people I care about and they've all come true in the past," Rachel disclosed.

"I have never gotten mad at you for anything, and I wouldn't get mad at you for sharing your feelings. I've known you since high school, and I never heard you speak about having a prophetic gift or anything of the sort," I challenged.

"It's a gift and a curse," Rachel explained. "Mel, it's all in his eyes. He's wearing a mask, hiding behind the Bible and whoever Myls is. He hides behind Myls because he doesn't like who he really is, or whoever Tory is, and I'm afraid you will get hurt."

I chuckled. "What do you think he's going to do, kill me or something?"

"No, I don't think he's going to kill you. He's mentally unstable. He will try to destroy you and compromise your mental health. But if you're not careful, somebody could die."

I was shocked to hear Rachel speak of Myls this way; she had never mentioned or given me any inclination of her disturbing thoughts about Myls before. She apologized again for putting those thoughts in my mind the night before the wedding and said that's why she had asked if I was sure I really wanted to know.

"Yeah," I replied, "but I didn't expect to hear you say that. I'm not upset. I respect your thoughts and concerns for me, but I don't have that same discernment about him." She seemed relieved.

"Good. Just pay attention to any red flags, and don't ignore them. I hope none of what I said or feel comes true. I'm here to support you no matter what. Tomorrow you are going to have a beautiful wedding. Don't stress about anything. Without a doubt, you are going be an amazing wife because you are an amazing person."

After the conversation, Rachel left to get ready for bed. That night, I decided not to call my fiancée Myls anymore, but to call him by his real name: Tory. I called Tory back, and we talked and prayed late into the midnight hours, never mentioning any of what Rachel and I had talked about.

chapter nine

THE WEDDING

Sunday, April 17, 2016 had arrived—the day I would marry my true love, my friend, my beautiful smile. It was a gorgeous, early spring day and things started on the right track. My maid of honor, Teresa, and makeup artist, Toi, rode with me to the wedding chapel and assisted me in getting ready. I didn't hire a wedding coordinator since we did the majority of the planning ourselves. I had asked a few people to assist with hosting, set up, and facilitating the flow of the day.

I typed up a step-by-step organized plan for the host to coordinate the flow of our wedding and reception. I was in constant communication with the bridal party, banquet staff, florist, baker, DJ, and photographer to be sure our requests and plans were aligned. Things seemed to be coming together, and the only thing I needed to be in complete peace was to know when my beautiful smile arrived.

While the bridesmaids and I were getting dressed and prepared, guests were starting to fill the chapel. Toi's music, soothing voice, and words of encouragement helped ease any anxious thoughts. Tory's sister, Marshon, one of our bridesmaids, came to me and said, "He is here; I laid eyes on him." Knowing my beautiful smile had arrived made my heart smile and I was ready to be Mrs. Smiles.

As I prepared to walk down the long vintage stairwell in my wedding gown with the long train cascading behind me, I heard the song "Love Was Made for Us" by Cleo playing. The bridal party began walking in, and that beautiful song brought tears to my eyes.

Looking at me, Toi's eyes lit up and she said softly, "No! Please don't cry," as she blotted tears away to keep my makeup intact. The song "I Found Love (Cindy's Song)" by BeBe & CeCe Winans began to play. The doors of the chapel opened, and I was greeted by my dad to walk me down the aisle to marry the man of my dreams.

Walking down the aisle, I was greeted and given away to this gorgeous, handsome man with the most beautiful smile. A reflection of the sun's rays beamed against his white tux, illuminating his face and sparkling teeth. We had a candlelight memorial honoring Tory's mother resting in heaven. Before God, family, and friends, we exchanged vows, rings, and kisses. I married that beautiful smile and became Mrs. Smiles.

The day felt like a dream come true, and I was the

happiest woman alive. The reception was absolutely beautiful: the table settings, decorations, wedding cake, and floral arrangements. The bridesmaids looked like princesses in their coral-colored dresses, and the groomsmen looked stunning in their tuxedos. Everything flowed as planned, and everyone seemed to be enjoying themselves. I couldn't have been happier to be married to someone I truly loved and who loved me.

Tory and I were thankful and blessed for all the love and support we were given, especially since the cost of our wedding almost tripled our initial set budget. Although our wedding and reception had come together beautifully, the day and time flew by quickly. I felt like Cinderella until the clock struck midnight and we headed home to prepare for our honeymoon.

The day after the wedding, we flew to Miami for our honeymoon cruise to the Bahamas. Tory had never been on a cruise ship before and was a little nervous about it. He said boats and water gave him anxiety because they reminded him of a scary accident years before when he fell off a jet ski into the Detroit River. After a word of prayer, Tory was less nervous. Our ship set sail, and we started our honeymoon journey.

We had a wonderful time relaxing and bonding, captivated by the beauty of the islands, clear blue water, and exotic fish. We went snorkeling and took excursions to private islands. We enjoyed every minute of it, and each other, without the interruptions of our phones, internet, or work. Tory couldn't stop talking about how beautiful everything was, from the cookies we received on the plane, to the excellent service, to the white sand he wanted to take home to remind him of the moments we had shared. Everything was like a fairytale dream come true.

chapter ten

THE MARRIAGE

Tory and I had discussed move-in plans early in our engagement and agreed to live in separate homes until we got married. I told Tory that once we were married, I was fine with living in either of our homes, and I left the decision to him. After the honeymoon was over, we immediately started packing and moved in together.

Being married and living together seemed to be going great. Tory still delivered flowers to my job, packed my lunch, and inserted love letters into my lunch bag. I woke up to love letters on our pillows and morning prayers. We read scriptures together and had fun date nights. After long days at work, Tory would run my bath water, and we gave one another massages almost weekly.

I would drive all over town to bring hot meals to his job

sites. Tory would call me throughout the day just to say he loved me or ask if I needed anything. He took care of all our home repairs, while I made sure the home was clean and he had clean labeled work uniforms daily. I arranged his appointments and made sure he got there on time. We made a list of our goals, assets, income, debts, household bills, and personal bills to collaborate and organize our expenses and ensure an efficient billing system that would help us meet our goals. There was effort on both ends to make sure needs were met, and there was balance in our household, love life, and finances.

Although our marriage seemed to be going well for several months, I still had a void and feelings of incompleteness that I thought marriage would take away. I began to wonder what the source of these feelings could be. I was working in my dream career field as a nurse, I was healthy, and our kids were healthy. We were not in a financial crisis or drowning in debt. My credit was good; I could get just about whatever I wanted. I had married the man of my dreams, who loved me, provided generously, and took good care of me. So why did I still feel empty and incomplete inside?

I mentioned my feelings to Tory and told him I felt spiritually deprived. I needed to get closer to the Lord. He said he understood because he had been there before. He wanted to support me in that area, but he didn't want his wife to become so holy that he couldn't enjoy me.

A few months after we got married, I started receiving cryptic messages and unusual calls at work from unknown callers who addressed me by my new married last name, which was odd because I hadn't notified many outside sources of my new last name yet. Initially, the callers would hang up as soon as I came to the phone. Then they started saying things about my husband and calling me names. They never said who they were, and I was never able to have a conversation without the caller prematurely yelling, cursing, and hanging up on me.

This went on for months, and I had no clue who it was or why they were doing this. I had never had these types of calls at work before. I didn't owe any debt collectors, and I didn't have any relationship issues with anyone. I mentioned it to Tory on several occasions, but he didn't seem to know who it could be or why they would be calling and saying those things about us. He believed it was someone I knew who might be low-key jealous of me.

The calls and harassment got worse, not only at work, but also on our house phone and my cell, and I was being harassed on social media. Someone created fake social media pages for me and my husband. They posted photos taken from our pages and our friends' and family members' social media pages. They posted wedding pictures I had never seen and made comments pretending to be me. They posted old pictures of my husband I had never seen before and shared information that none of our family or friends knew about.

At the time, I guess I wasn't responding or entertaining them the way they wanted me to, so the calls and harassment got worse. One of the callers said, "Thanks for the house, b#*@h. I will see you when we come back from out of town," before laughing and hanging up on me. They would say things that would strike a thought related to actual situations that had happened, like a text message that read, "And where was he the night before your wedding?" Another text said, "If I catch you driving any of my cars, I'mma call the police on yo' a**!"

Some of those calls and texts left unsettling feelings in my stomach and questionable thoughts. My discernment had increased, and I was more alert and watchful of things going on around me and in my marriage. I informed my coworkers not to transfer or relay any outside calls to me. Unable to get me on the phone at work, the hostile caller began talking about me or my husband to whomever answered the phone. I often shared the incidents with Tory, but he continued denying knowing who it was.

One day, while talking to Tory about the calls and messages, he said it could be any of our exes. I recalled him telling me a while back about a woman named Sherry, whom he had dated for a short time prior to meeting me. Tory said he had stopped talking to Sherry because she was crazy and had a hard time letting go; he revealed he'd had to call the police on her a while back. Apparently, she kept coming over unannounced after Tory told her not to and told her he had moved on and was about to get married. He said she got upset, started banging her head on her steering wheel, running over his trash cans, and threatening to slash his tires and bust out his windows if he didn't leave me and get back with her. Tory said they arrested her and sent her to jail.

"Whatever happened to the lady you said was crazy and you called the police on?" I asked.

"I don't know, but I don't think it's her," Tory answered. "She's in the past, and I haven't heard anything from her since I sent her to jail." He also said he blocked her number and that she never knew my name or anything about me. "I still think it's somebody you know, or someone you've been talking to. Baby, you have to understand. Now that we are married, the adversary is mad and is going to try to come in between us any way he can. That's why it's important that we cover one another in prayer and not let anyone come in between what God put together. Not everybody is happy about us being married, Melanie, including the ones that say they are and smile in your face—they want what we have, and it's our job to protect our marriage and one another."

Our family members and friends started telling us they were getting messages and being harassed with inappropriate comments and videos about Tory and me on social media. Some of the videos were very disturbing and a couple were YouTube videos of women talking about Tory, calling him names and accusing him of promiscuous behavior. Some of the women were claiming his last name on their social media pages, acknowledging they were engaged or had been in a relationship with him. A woman in one of the videos warned other women to stay away from my husband, accusing him of being a slumlord and liar who engaged in illegal activity and used women. She identified herself as Leah Forson. That name sounded so familiar.

I decided to investigate and find out who these people

were and what was really going on. One day, my friend Rachel called, and somewhere in our conversation I mentioned the calls and messages I had been receiving. Once again, she gave me that loud silence.

"That's it," Rachel said.

"What's it?" I asked.

"The vison I shared with you the night before the wedding is connected to the calls," Rachel said. "Be careful. People are crazy these days. I could be wrong, but I believe Tory is the reason you are getting those calls."

I didn't understand why Rachel had such a strong misunderstanding of Tory. I questioned her feelings about him once again, and hoped that in time, her thoughts of him would be proven wrong.

It didn't take long for me to figure out who Leah Forson was. I thought back to our drive to Alabama when I was pulled over for speeding in Tory's new Mercedes Benz. The cop had asked me about Leah Forson. That's whose name the car was in. I confronted Tory about all this, and he said Leah Forson was one of his past tenants who had a crush on him. He said the videos were old, made and posted years before we met. He assured me he and Leah had never dated.

"Is the Mercedes I've been driving still in her name?" I inquired. Tory looked surprised as if he didn't think I remembered.

"No. The car is not in her name anymore. Melanie, you and I were not engaged when I bought that car. Leah helped me out before, and I trusted her to do it again. I asked you to put the car in your name, but you wouldn't."

"We weren't engaged when you bought the car," I inserted, "but we *were* dating and in a committed relationship. You never mentioned anything else about putting the car in my name until now when I just brought it up."

"Baby, you are my wife, and I told you whatever I have is yours," Tory began. "When we got pulled over, I told you I hadn't had the chance to change the title and that you could put it in your name. You didn't do it. I shouldn't have to keep asking you for things you know I need, and I don't want to have to ask anyone else for things I know you can do."

We went back and forth until he got upset and decided to give me the silent treatment again. It hadn't been a year yet since we got married, and it had been one thing after another. Once I found out who Leah Forson was, our marriage quickly took a turn for the worse. The harassing calls continued almost daily, and I was getting pissed off at the persistent harsh accusations, lies, disrespect, and stress afflicted upon My family and me for no known reason. It got to the point where our family, friends, and kids were also engaging back and forth in the calls and social media chaos.

In August of that year, Tory and I went to Atlanta for Rachel's birthday gathering to have some time away together. We had a good time enjoying our friends. Tory's sister, Marshon, and his brother-in-law drove in from Alabama to join us. It was a relaxing and stress-free getaway until I decided to login to social media. My news feed was flooded with missing person pictures, posts, and alerts about my daughter's best friend, Jacqueline, whom we call "Shug." Shug is also my grandson's godmother.

In shock, thinking this couldn't be real, I immediately called Shug's sister, Krissy, asking about the posts. She informed me the posts were true and that no one had seen or heard from Jacqueline since yesterday, which was unlike her. Krissy was on her way to the police station and would update me later.

Hours later, Krissy called me back, and I will never forget hearing her terrifying cry, telling me Shug was found shot dead in the backyard of a vacant home. My heart dropped, and I almost fell to the floor.

This was a devastating loss and horrific tragedy for Shug's family, the community, and my daughter. A precious life taken away much too soon by some evildoer she thought she could trust. Shug would've turned twenty-two years old the following month. My daughter fell into a serious depression and was unable to cope with life after Shug's death. Shug was my daughter's right hand, who spoke logic and reason into her. They had been best friends since they were in diapers. Shug was working as a medical assistant and was looking forward to becoming a nurse.

After the painful loss of Shug, my stepdad's health suddenly took a turn for the worse. My stepdad and mom had been married for almost thirty years, and this was a sad and stressful season for us all. Just days after Thanksgiving, my sister received a call from the hospital notifying us of a decline in Dad's condition and requested to have the family come to the hospital. When I arrived at the hospital and entered his room, he was unresponsive with cold extremities. The ventilator was breathing for him and the cardiac monitor displayed a weak, low heart rate. That's when I knew in my heart that heaven's doors had opened for him and his days of suffering were now over.

In that moment, still at my dad's bedside, I received a text message from an unknown number with several pictures of my husband and other women. Some were pictures of him hugged up with other women. Another picture was taken from a social media post of him and another woman horseback riding, dated around my birthday. I remembered that was around the time Tory got upset about something and gave me the silent treatment for days, even on my birthday. Along with other pictures was a message attached saying, "Your husband, our man, is cheating on both of us, and he just left my house."

Later that evening, Dad passed away. Although thoughts of those texts messages were festering, my main concern at that time was for my mom and siblings. I grieved and tried to remain strong for my family. The first Christmas ever without our dad made it one of the toughest holiday seasons to endure. Tory was sympathetic, compassionate, and supportive of my family and me during that difficult time.

I eventually showed Tory the text messages and pictures. He got upset, saying they were all lies.

"Those pictures were taken before I met you," he explained. "You always know where I am. I'm home every night. Stop feeding into their mess. I married who I wanted, and they're just mad and jealous I'm not with them."

It wasn't until later on I thought about the time we went

horseback riding for Tory's birthday in Traverse City. He had told me then that was his first time riding a horse, but that couldn't have been true if the pictures were old. Things didn't feel right, and I was determined to find out who was behind this and what was going on.

chapter eleven

MY BROKEN SMILES

The holiday season was over and Tory and I started the new year off with a court case involving a couple of his rental properties. I could sense Tory's anxiety and increased agitation the closer it came to his court date. I remained supportive and obtained a good defense attorney for his case, but court didn't go exactly how Tory wanted. He didn't get the worse punishment, but he had to serve one week of jail time. They booked him right after court to start serving his one-week sentence. I felt sad and helpless as I watched them remove Tory's belongings and take him away. Even though it was only for a week, I cried all the way home, praying they treated him okay in there.

The crying didn't last long at all. When I got home, I found another parking citation on our door for one of Tory's work trucks parked on the grass in the backyard. I moved the truck from the backyard to our driveway and upon getting out the truck, I heard a phone ring. I looked around and found Tory's cell phone, thinking he must have forgotten his phone was in the truck. The phone kept ringing, and I hardly ever heard his phone ring. I recognized some of the names calling and decided to answer in case it was one of the tenants. I also wanted to know why there were so many unfamiliar female callers. I wasn't prepared for the mortal blow and overwhelming force that shot through my heart and plunged into my gut from answering those calls. It was like a nuclear bomb had just gone off in my life.

The first call I answered was from a woman named Tia, who was taken by surprise at me answering Tory's phone. She wanted to know who I was. I told her I was Mrs. Smiles, Tory's wife, and that he was unavailable at the moment.

"How can I help you?" I asked.

"His wife? How's that possible? We've been dating for three years. He has keys to my house, and his kids know me. I was calling to see how court went."

While I was talking to Tia, another call beeped in, a woman named Ms. Shiny. She said she knew Tory was married, but that he took care of her and her kids, and Tory had told her she was his soulmate.

Within a few minutes, Leah Forson called, yelling and screaming and asking why I was answering Tory's phone. She warned that I better not be driving any of her cars or she was going to call the police. A different girl named Tia called and said she and Tory had an on-and-off relationship because he was always lying and going MIA. In his contacts, I saw names like "Home Depot Diamond" and "Home Depot Red," both of whom had texted how much they loved and missed Tory. Some of these girls were younger than our children, texting half-nude, inappropriate pictures. A young woman named Samiya asked if he was still coming to take her to school.

There were current texts messages from Sherry, the woman Tory called crazy and claimed he hadn't spoken to or seen since he called the police on her. He was telling most of these women he loved them, and they were expressing their deepest love for him. Another woman who called said she didn't know Tory was married because he continued to bring her around his family, and the family knew the two of them were in a relationship. She even named the family members, dates, and occasions. Other contacts like "Beauchamp niece, Dana," "Ms. Coffee," "Shonte," "Angie," and several others sent intimate messages and pictures. The calls and texts kept coming all day and night.

My head was pounding. I began hyperventilating. I was sweating profusely, my heart was racing, and I was nauseated. Overtaken by despair, I had to shut the phone off to suppress the emotional strangulation. Racing thoughts of anger and disbelief saturated my mind all night. How? Why? When? I didn't get a moment of sleep and had to call off work the next day. I spent the next couple of days visiting my OB/GYN and getting checked out. It was so embarrassing to share my situation with her, but I needed to be sure I was still healthy, in spite of my unfaithful husband.

I began investigating the accusations of these women and anything else I might have overlooked or ignored throughout my relationship with Tory. I went into CSI mode, googling, searching social media sites and paid websites. I also contacted people I knew who could help investigate this situation.

While Tory was in jail, I went to all our rental homes to collect rent, and to speak to and get to know the tenants. Most of them said they didn't know Tory was married and complained they were never able to reach him for much needed repairs until it was time to pay rent. Others complained of being unable to get utilities turned on due to illegal use or from previous tenants' outstanding bills. I found out some of Tory's female tenants had prior and current intimate relationships with him and didn't pay him any rent.

I found the titles to all the cars, trucks, and motorcycles. I was in shock to see that several of our vehicles, houses, and motorcycles were in Leah Forson's and several other people's names. I found restraining orders that Tory had served to multiple women, including the woman, Sherry, whom he called the police on and gone horseback riding with. Another restraining order was for a girl who intruded upon him while he was in the house with another girl. The incident reports on all the restraining orders involved women he had relationships with and how they reacted to finding out he cheated on or hurt them. Reading the incident details was disturbing. Those women were clearly hurt by Tory cheating on them, which caused them to react emotionally in unsettling ways.

Not only did Tory hurt these women, he had some of them arrested and served them restraining orders for situations *he* created. I found a heart-wrenching card and letter from a woman named Angel, confessing her love for him but saying she could no longer live with the pain Tory had caused her. She signed the letter, "Love, your wife, Angel." He had been married more than once before me.

I was blown away and in disbelief from all the information revealed to me. I was plotting how I was going to knock him out when I picked him up from jail. I wondered if he called, should I tell him or wait until he got out? I had so much rage, anger, and pain, and so many questions. How could a so-called man of God do this to his wife and other women? What could I have done to make him do this to me?

I hadn't spoken to Tory since he went to jail and only communicated with him through his lawyer. He completed his seven-day jail sentence, and I was outside waiting for him to come out. In my head, I was still practicing how I was going to knock him out and tell him what I had discovered. I didn't want to go to jail, so I decided to wait until we were off the jail premises.

My hands were sweaty and my head and heart were pounding. Tory got into the car, hugging me and happy to see me. I wanted to see if he knew or showed any signs of me knowing. As we drove off, Tory told me about his jail experience and how thankful he was for me and my support. I knew then he didn't have a clue about the hell and misery I had trampled through the past week.

About five minutes into our drive home, I couldn't hold back any longer.

I calmly said, "I found your phone in the red truck. I answered the calls, too. I couldn't believe all the stuff my husband is out here doing."

"Baby, what are you talking about?" Tory asked innocently.

"You know exactly what I'm talking about!" I let loose. "I married a nasty, trifling, no-good, lying, dirty dog hypocrite! I spoke to all the Tias, Nias, Samiya, Tanzy, and Home Depot chicks you've been seeing. Some of them said you are taking care of their kids! You claim you don't like kids, but you do a good job of playing daddy to other people's kids you don't like!" His eyes lit up like he had seen a ghost. He had the nerve to deflect.

"Why did you answer my phone?" Tory demanded. That response just poured gasoline over the flame already burning inside me, almost making me run into the median on the freeway. I started crying, hitting Tory out of anger, asking him why and how he could do this. He reached for the steering wheel.

"You're acting crazy. You're going to kill us!" I came to an unknown exit and stopped the truck abruptly, continuing to express my emotions and tell him the things I had found out. Tory shifted the focus back onto me.

"Do you see how you are acting? I can't handle you like this. You're striking me and trying to get us killed. I can't answer any of your questions if we end up dead." Tory begged me to calm down. "Baby, look, I messed up. I know you're upset. I hurt you. I let you down. But trust me, those women mean nothing to me; I only used them for what they could do for me."

Tory tried to convince me he only used the women for things he needed when I wouldn't do for him or make time to do what he needed.

"Please don't believe half of what they told you," he pleaded. "Yes, I have keys to some of their houses. If they're living in *my* house, I need access in case something happens. That's why I have all those keys on my key ring. I don't tell people I'm married because they don't need to be in my business. They don't even know my real name. That's why I tell them my name is Myls, so they can't go looking me up. It's to protect us while I'm in these streets working.

"Please don't believe what they told you. I'm sure you told them some things that hurt them, too. After you answered my phone and told them I was married, of course they're going to tell you things to hurt you. I probably did tell them I love them, and I was wrong for that. I can easily tell people I love them and not mean a word of it. I can do that to people I don't care anything about, but you should never question my love for you. I never loved anyone as much as I love you."

Everything Tory said was making me feel worse. I kept wondering how could he look me dead in my eyes and still be lying. I wanted to punch him in those lying lips and shut him up.

"Doll, I will do whatever it takes to make this right with you," Tory begged. "I will call each one of the women and apologize to them right now in front of you, and let them know whatever they thought we had is over. Whatever I have to do to secure your insecurities, I'm going to do it."

He asked if we could go to marriage counseling and told me he needed help in other areas. Tory begged me not to leave him and said he would do whatever it took to right the wrong. He said he would get the cars transferred out of Leah Forson's name and asked me to go with him to the Secretary of State to show proof. I told him I needed space and wanted him to go to a doctor and get checked out.

Tory called a couple of the women in front of me, apologizing for misleading and lying to them. He said he loved his wife and didn't mean to hurt me or anyone else. He found a clinic on Woodward that did rapid testing and came back with a clean bill of health and results. That wasn't enough for me, though. I scheduled him a full physical and blood work with my primary doctor, and he also went there for testing.

I had always heard the first couple years of marriage are the hardest. Keeping that in mind, I did what I thought was best to save our marriage. I searched and found a marriage counselor for us to start counseling sessions.

Despite Tory's best effort at getting help and trying to right his wrongs, the trust was broken in our marriage. I knew it would take time and work to fix this. The psychological effects of his actions and betrayal lingered, and I constantly monitored his behavior, whereabouts, and work schedules and locations. I started reading and listening to more spiritually empowering books and audio. I frequently visited massage spas and regularly went to the park to walk and exercise. I tried to involve us in anything that could help heal or build within our marriage.

We attended marriage counseling together, and although none of the therapists were successful in helping us, I admired Tory's desire to keep seeking help and showing me how important our marriage was to him. He suggested we seek counseling together as a couple and expressed that he wanted to seek individual counseling for himself.

I thought that finally my prayers were being answered. Tory and I were taking frequent trips, vacations, and cruises together. We registered a business together where we bought homes with cash and fixed them up as rental investments. At times, I would go over to the rental properties and help him. He was coming home on time and notifying me of his whereabouts. He would even ask me what time I'd like him to be home, and whatever time I said, he was sure to be home at that time.

Tory would ask me to come to work with him, saying, "I want my wife to know where I am and never have to worry about me being with another woman." He would ask me to bring him lunch, telling me he was not really hungry but just wanted to see me since it would make his day much better. He would call me and say he just wanted to hear my beautiful voice. Tory would often say he knew he was a piece of work and not the easiest person to put up with, but he was thankful for me not giving up on our marriage. He said I was his blessing from God.

Tory continued to write me love letters and secretly stash them in my lunch bag, confessing his love for me and saying all the right things. He would surprise me with "just because" gifts. One day, I came home to a new pink motorcycle. He'd stop by the mall and buy me two or three bottles of designer perfume, new handbags, work shoes, and sexy outfits.

Tory assured me I didn't have to worry about him talking to other women anymore because God was about to use what we had gone through for a powerful testimony and ministry. He said he knew God was calling him to preach, but he wanted us to be ready and developed. He ministered and prayed for whomever needed a word. People would call on Tory daily for prayer, encouragement, money, or spiritual guidance like he was their savior.

Although our marriage started out as an emotional roller coaster, I was starting to feel like we were getting back on track. I was ready to dive back in; shower him with selfless, unlimited love; and fulfill my role as a virtuous wife. I was once again ready to give Tory and this marriage my best and make God proud.

Tory had me feeling like I was in a love fantasy. He implemented frequent evaluations of our marriage and his behaviors. He would invite me to see his work and request my input. Tory began to do things in an abnormal, excessive way, even when I showed gratitude or told him he was doing a good job. "Good isn't good enough," he would say. "You deserve great! I want to give you my best."

Tory would ask me if he could go places and ask what time his curfew was. I wasn't sure if he was being sarcastic or if he was really trying to secure my trust in him. It got to the point where I began telling him, "It's okay. Go and enjoy yourself. You don't have to do all that now." Feeling as if Tory had proven himself trustworthy, I no longer needed to be love-bombed and apologized to so constantly.

Since things were going okay for the moment, Tory came up with an idea to earn extra money with our travel business by doing vacation marriage ministries. I told him I hoped we could eventually do that, but I didn't feel our marriage was strong or stable enough at the time to help other married couples. I didn't feel comfortable doing it then.

"If we haven't consistently managed or developed our marriage," I asked, "how can we lead a marriage ministry?"

Tory gave me the look of the devil himself. "I can't get you to do anything! Why can't you just do what I asked? *You* wear the pants in the house. It's a shame I can't depend on my wife to do what I ask her to do or follow my lead," he replied, hostile.

"There isn't anything I wouldn't do for you," I said. "I believe I'm a reliable source for you, and I've proven that on many occasions. You're thinking about how much money we could make, but ministry is serving, doing work of the Lord, and allowing him to use you as a vessel for his people. We have to lead by example. We can't just hear or know the Word, but we have to apply it and live it! How can we fix somebody else's broken marriage when we haven't fixed our own?" I asked Tory to name a time when he needed me to do something and I didn't do it. He came up with only two things: putting a Home Depot credit card in my name and buying a sixty-thousand-dollar work truck.

We had about four good, working, drivable trucks and

over ten cars when he asked me to buy a new truck. He had refused to drive one of the pickup trucks for work because he said it was too nice to work in and he didn't want to mess it up. To me, it didn't make sense to buy another vehicle at the time.

"Tory," I explained, "early in the marriage, I submitted graciously to following your God-given role to lead, until I found out about all the lies and cheating. I am your helper, here to build with you, but it's hard for me to submit to someone I can't trust. I need you to lead this family, just not the way you've been doing it."

Months later, the harassing calls and threats were still coming to my job. I learned that a woman came to my job on one of my off days, making complaints and false accusations against me and my husband. I had never met or seen the person my coworkers described. She approached one of my coworkers and began harassing her, thinking she was me. After an investigation was done, her allegations were proven false and fabricated. Tory demanded I also file a police report on the woman, whom I learned was Leah Forson. He drove me to the police station and gave me and the police Leah's information to file the report. The restraining order was granted, and Leah was served immediately.

Shortly after that, someone called Tory and told him one of his rental properties was on fire. A dissatisfied tenant had moved out and expressed her anger by setting the house on fire. Not only was there major fire damage, the house was trashed and had what appeared to be multiple bullet holes in the walls, busted windows, a ripped out electrical box, and water damage from a faucet left running for an unknown period of time. Another tenant Tory had dated poured bleach on the floors, broke windows, knocked holes in the walls, and trashed the house upon moving out. They left nothing to the imagination about how mad they were. You would think Tory had learned his lesson about relationships with women renting his homes, especially while he was married.

The harassing calls at work eventually stopped, but other things began to surface at home. A couple months after we served Leah with the restraining order, I found a signed land contract agreement between my husband, Leah, and one other person at one of our rental properties dated only two months *after* we served her the restraining order. My heart hit the floor again in disbelief. I felt betrayed.

When I asked Tory about it, he got upset and told me it was only business, and he wasn't turning down twenty-two hundred dollars a month. I couldn't believe what he had said, as if I cared about how much money she was paying. I told him it was not about the money; it was about what she had done to me and about his loyalty to me—his wife.

He said I was always trying to control him, which wasn't true. He tried to justify his wrongs and act like he did nothing wrong.

"We have an active restraining order on her!" I cried.

"No," Tory said. "*You* have a restraining order on her." It felt like somebody hit me in my chest and I was about to pass out. "I'm not about to let you tell me how to run my business. You can't possibly think I want Leah. She has a boyfriend who works for me, and I have a business to run.

"*She's* the reason you're getting all those flowers and nice gifts. *She's* the one paying the mortgage on this house, just like all the others who are renting from us and making us money. You really should be thanking her and be glad she accepted your apology."

"What the hell are you talking about? What apology?" I felt like I was going crazy.

"I told her you were sorry for putting the restraining order on her," Tory replied.

"Why the heck would you do that? And why would I apologize after what she's done? I never did anything to that woman! She came at me for something *you* did to her."

"I told her you were sorry to calm her down, to save your job, and to run my business," Tory replied calmly. "You have more to lose than she does; she doesn't have anything to lose. Didn't it work? She hasn't been calling or bothering you, has she?"

I was furious, disgusted, and devastated by what Tory had said. I wanted to spit in his face. His eyes began to squint—that demonic look in his eyes and face that I had grown accustomed to. This time, I thought I saw horns. The more I tried to explain how wrong he was, the more hurtful and confusing Tory became, leaving me with a terrible migraine and sickness in my stomach.

Once again, he gave me the silent treatment as punishment for something he had done to me, this time longer than the last. I had started getting used to the silence and used that time to gather my thoughts and process things. He would leave out for work at the break of day and be gone until midnight. He would leave on his motorcycle and disappear. I wouldn't hear from him the entire day and he wouldn't answer his phone. Tory became more disrespectful and emotionally abusive. I asked him to move out.

Tory moved into one of our vacant rental homes, but only took a few of his belongings. We didn't communicate for a couple months. During that separation period, I received calls from an unknown caller who would prompt a toddler to say, "Where's my daddy? Tell my daddy to call me back. I love you, Daddy." I didn't mention it to Tory because I didn't feel like suffering another devastation or fight with him. People would see him out with other women and take photos and send them to me via text or social media.

His way of reaching out to me was sending me a text to ask if he could come by and grab clothes or work equipment. When he came over, he said we needed to talk and get an understanding of things.

"What is it you don't understand?" I demanded. "I understand you are a lying, cheating, evil, and deceitful man. You are allergic to normalcy. I don't want to hear another one of your sorry apologies. No one is sorry for something they keep doing to you, knowing they're hurting you. I've been patient with you, loved you through your mess, and tried to get us help. You would think a person would be more caring, apologetic, and empathetic toward you after you've forgiven and taken them back after they hurt you. You're always saying I'm your soulmate, but you are not giving me what my soul needs. This is more like a soul-tie or trauma bond, which is the opposite of a soulmate. My soul needs respect, love, honesty, and peace, which I will not compromise on, and which should have been the foundation of our marriage."

Tory apologized but never seemed able to properly show his remorse. At times, it appeared he intentionally did things he knew would hurt me. It seemed when things were going good, he found a way to create drama or instability. He constantly wanted attention, validation, and admiration from others but went about getting it the wrong way. He accused me of verbally abusing him when we would argue and said my words hurt him just as badly as his actions had hurt me.

He compared expressing my feelings about his bad behaviors to his many lies, his cheating, and his deceptions. He said his lying and cheating weren't any worse than me calling him names, even if I only did it because he hurt me. "Pain is pain," Tory said, "and wrong is wrong in the eyes of the Lord." He always quoted scripture behind it.

Tory told me the Lord had been talking to him about getting help during our separation. He would apologize to no end and say God was taking us though some things for a reason, and he believed these were just tests and we could get through them. He begged me not to give up on our marriage; he asked me to be there for him and help find him a therapist. He said he didn't know why he continued to do wrong and hurt people. He said he carried the spirit of abandonment because everyone he loves leaves him. He said there had been times when he wanted to commit suicide after we argued, and he really wanted to get help.

I could sense the constant war Tory was battling in his mind with the enemy, and hearing my husband express thoughts of not wanting to live after we argued hurt me. I felt sad, and feelings of guilt started to emerge from within me. Although he had hurt me, my soul would be crushed if something like that happened to him. I was intentional about getting my husband help.

Tory showed dedication to therapy. He was on time and participated in the sessions. While Tory was in therapy, he and his boys started communicating in hopes of building a stronger relationship. I enjoyed talking to them and being in their lives. Alaysia became one of the sweetest stepdaughters anyone could ask for. Tory had some amazing, wise, talented, and gifted kids. In a short amount of time, I developed a love and relationship with a few of them that I never wanted to lose.

Counseling wasn't effective, though, because Tory had a hard time being vulnerable, opening up, and answering questions honestly. I noticed one of the therapists was frustrated and didn't believe some of Tory's answers. Tory began saying the therapists didn't care about us and just wanted our money.

Things were still up and down between Tory and me. I was constantly thinking that if we could just get over this problem, if we could just fix this, or if he could just change, or stop doing that, things would be perfect. He told me he wanted to keep a safe house because our relationship had him walking on eggshells. He wanted to keep some of his belongings at the house he stayed at when we separated.

"A safe house?" I asked. "You can forget a safe house. It may be best and safer for you to stay over there."

A social media friend of mine reached out to me and told me she had seen my husband out, booed up with one of her clients. She sent me photos. I also found out he was talking to a women named Sherry and a woman named Ms. Jones from our travel company. When we went to Florida for one of our travel conferences, both women were there, but at that time I only knew of one of them.

Women were still coming out left and right. It was unbelievable. I found out Tory had furnished the house he stayed in when we separated, moved his uncle in, and would bring many different women over there. Some of the women couldn't believe he was married because he had mastered the lie and deception so well.

I had no idea whom I was married to, and every incident was getting worse than the last. I finally told Tory, "My mind and body are no longer safe with you. You are creating masses of soul-ties and sex-ties. I can't be intimate with you again, and the thought of you touching me makes my soul cringe."

"That's fine," he said nonchalantly, "because I'm tired of you making me go back and forth to the doctor to prove I don't have anything. Don't ask me to do nothing else." I told him we wouldn't have these issues if he wasn't community property and everybody's man.

I informed some of the women I knew about of Tory's infidelity, letting them know he was not the man he was pretending to be. Some didn't care as long as they were getting what they wanted. Tory was so charming and a master of his craft. Loving him was like an addiction that was bad for the mind, body, and spirit. I knew eventually they would share the same experience of a broken smile.

When Tory realized I was truly tired and done, and wasn't giving into anymore of his schemes, he started spiraling out of control. He no longer hid being reckless and criminal-minded, and he openly engaged in unhealthy behaviors. People accused him of ripping them off and not completing already-paid projects. He tried to accuse me of cheating and talking to other men after I mentioned having a spiritual conversation with a male childhood friend.

He said, "If you want to see other people, you better look out the window."

"You're creating things in your mind that aren't true," I defended. "*You're* the cheater, not me! I'm not like you or those other women. I never have and never will cheat on my husband. I have respect for myself, and I will divorce you before I cheat."

Tory was so convinced I was cheating that he threatened to kill me and anyone around me. I recorded his threats as he began explaining why he would kill me. Tory said he loved me so much, despite what he had done to me, that he couldn't handle me being with another man. I told him I didn't know him anymore and that he appeared to be two different people.

"It's actually four," Tory said calmly.

"Four of what?" I asked, confused.

"I have four different sides of me. Four different people."

He looked at me then he turned and looked at the television and said, "Just like that TV. That TV has four different sides: two sides, a front and a back, but we can only see the front side that is facing us. That's exactly how I am."

Stunned, I said, "I didn't know there were four of you."

"We all have different sides of us," Tory declared.

I started seeing that demonic spirit in Tory's face more often. I didn't feel safe around him anymore, and I told members of his family about his erratic behaviors and threats. I was tired of sleeping with my bedroom door locked and my glock at my right hand, and I was tired of spending nights with other family members just to stay away from Tory. Things had gotten out of hand with him more than once; the police were called, and I filed a report. I found and removed about ten guns from the house. I was finally able to safely separate and get Tory to completely remove all his things, and himself, from the house.

Just when I thought my heart couldn't take any more, I received an email from Carnival Cruise Lines saying, "Congratulations, Melanie and Tory! Thanks for booking with us. We look forward to cruising with you in fifty-two days!" At first I thought it must be spam or an advertisement because I hadn't booked anything. But the email had my membership information, booking number, and a complete itinerary of a paid-in-full, seven-day Western Caribbean cruise to Belize, Mahogany Bay, Grand Cayman Islands, and Cozumel. Guest information and passenger names listed were my husband and a woman named Dana who had contacted me months before saying she had just found out Tory was married and a liar. She said Tory told her his wife had passed away. Dana thought they were in a real relationship, and she sent me pictures of them at concerts, dinner, and the zoo, where he had helped chaperone her class field trip. She also said she had just divorced a cheating husband and would never date a married man. When we talked, Dana told me she was blocking Tory and would never talk to him again. I didn't really believe she was done with him because that's what they all said.

I figured Tory and Dana would be excited and looking forward to their vacation to the beautiful islands in the Caribbean. I didn't bother saying anything about it right away, plotting my revenge. I'm sure Tory was tired from work, the stress of another failing marriage, living multiple lives, and all the running back and forth with different women. The trip was booked during school winter break, and I figured Dana wanted to use that time to break free of her stressors of being a school teacher and dealing with Tory's schemes.

Since they used my travel information and included me on their email, I simply logged in and removed all Dana's information and replaced it with mine. After I made the changes and received my confirmation via email, I called the cruise line to put a password on the booking and told them not to make any more adjustments without contacting me first.

After giving them enough time to plan and get all excited about their trip, I cancelled the entire trip close to the departure date and after the refund period passed.

chapter twelve

TRANSFORMATION/ BEAUTIFULLY BROKEN

As things got worse in my marriage, my attitude also got worse. I felt like I was mentally changing into a new creature under Satan's influence. I didn't like me, and it seemed as if Tory's spirit had become a host within me. I was reacting with so much anger, rage, and emotion. In one of our arguments, Tory said I was not the same sweet little princess he married. I told him it was his fault and he should be mad at himself because this was what he had created and birthed. I was angry that he didn't value the love of family and chose to fill his life with women, money, and lust. I was angry I married someone heartless, soulless, and deceptive. I was angrier that the pain stopped me from being the loving, respectful, and supportive wife I desired to be. Instead of growing and learning to love my new husband, I ended up learning and studying my opponent. I married a broken smile—a covert, narcissistic, sociopathic spirit that mimicked the python, Jezebel, and Leviathan spirits all in one. Almost every area of my life was infected, from my marriage and home to my work, business, and family.

I had suffered from headaches and migraines for years, but they were coming more frequently and lasting longer. I began having bouts of dizziness with my headaches, which was unusual. I took my blood pressure, and it read 214/110. I was shocked. I'd never had high blood pressure, and I visited my doctors regularly for routine exams and checkups. I was also pretty active. My blood pressure was at stroke level, and I was a walking time bomb.

I was taking braids out of my hair one day when I noticed large patches of my own hair coming out. The more I combed, the more came out. I was devastated and when I took pictures and showed my family, they were in disbelief as well. My nails were brittle, my face was breaking out, and I always felt tired. Everything happening on the inside of me was starting to reflect outwardly.

My son developed a sudden episode of bipolar depression and was admitted to a crisis center. My daughter went through cycles of depression and couldn't provide basic needs for my grandson due to difficulty coping with the death of her best friend, Shug. My mom, myself, and siblings were grieving the loss of my stepdad, and I felt like I had to be strong for us all. Throughout all this, I kept a smile on my face. I continued to pray and go to church, asking others to pray for us and praying God would fix things, but nothing changed. Life was weighing on me.

I was still getting calls, texts, and information about Tory. Thinking about all the new and exciting things I had introduced into Tory's life, I saw that he was now doing them with other women. I was never suicidal, but I was potentially homicidal from the pain and threats caused by him and fear of the unknown. I just wanted the pain to stop. I was overwhelmed, stressed to the max, drained, and depleted. At this point, it felt like I was losing my mind, and I feared having a nervous breakdown. The revelation Rachel spoke of the night before my wedding continued to play over and over in my mind. It seemed as if I was watching a previously recorded Lifetime movie unfold. I knew I couldn't win this on my own, but I didn't want to be seen or bothered by anyone. I wanted to isolate myself in darkness until the pain in my soul disappeared. My spirit was crushed, and I was in desperate need of God.

One day, as I was standing in the shower feeling mentally and physically drained, with nothing left to give, I started crying. I needed help. I wanted God to help me, heal me, change my heart, and make me better. I was ready to surrender it all. My heart was racing, and I started calling on the Lord. I screamed at the top of my lungs, "Lord, where are you? I need you! Please help me. Come see about me! I don't want to be like this anymore!"

I cried harder and screamed louder until my voice became hoarse. My legs became weaker, and before I knew it, I slipped and fell on the bathtub floor. That fall quickly stopped all the crying and hollering I was doing. I didn't get up right away. I just lay there looking stupid, buck naked, with one leg hanging out of the tub, the shower curtain hanging down, and shower water running all over me. As I lay there, I felt a wind of calm resting over me, and I heard the sound of a soft inner voice whisper, "Now you're ready."

I began to calm down, exhausted but feeling comforted and relieved by a sudden sense of peace. I was still on the bathtub floor with water running over my face as if it were washing my tears away. After a few minutes, I got up out the shower to grab my cell phone and speaker. Walking naked through the house, unbothered by the cool air that hit my wet body or the tracks of water on the floor, I walked back to the shower to play some music. The song "Change Me" by Tamela Mann was on my mind, and that was the first song I played on YouTube. After listening to a few songs, an audio version of the Book of Proverbs came on. As much as I listened to sermons, I had never listened to an audio scripture reading. I thought about changing to another gospel song to stay in that peaceful and uplifting state, but I didn't feel like getting back up, so I let it play. I heard things like "for gaining wisdom and instruction," "for understanding words of insight," "to receive instruction," "doing what is right and fair," and "let the wise listen and let the discerning get guidance." Then I heard,

"The fear of the Lord is the beginning of knowledge,
but fools despise wisdom and instruction."

(PROVERBS 1:7 NIV)

Those words caught my attention. I kept listening. At the end of that first chapter, I heard,

"But whoever listens to me will live in safety and
be at ease, without fear of harm."

(PROVERBS 1:33 NIV)

After listening to that first chapter, it felt like the Lord was talking to me and I was ready to listen. I couldn't help but think of Tory and relate some of those scriptures to him. After I cried out loud to the Lord in the shower, surrendered to him, and asked for his help, Proverbs chapter two confirmed what I needed to do and the benefits of seeking Godly wisdom.

"Indeed, if you call out for insight and cry aloud
for understanding, and if you look for it as for
silver and search for it as for hidden treasure, then
you will understand the fear of the Lord and find the
knowledge of God."

(PROVERBS 2:3–5 NIV)

To be honest, it kind of spooked me a little as I looked around for signs of God's presence, feeling He had heard my cry and led me to hear this. I had mental flashes and thoughts of my broken smile and his behaviors as I associated him with significant words, actions, and characteristics of these scriptures. I heard,

> "*Wisdom will save you from the ways of wicked men, from men whose words are perverse, who have left the straight paths to walk in the dark ways, who delight in doing wrong and rejoice in the perverseness of evil, whose paths are crooked and who are devious in their ways. Wisdom will save you also from the adulterous woman, from the wayward woman with her seductive words, who has left the partner of her youth and ignored the covenant she made before God.*"
>
> (PROVERBS 2:12–17 NIV)

I saw my broken smile in these scriptures as they reflected his actions and ignored the covenant he and I made before God. Any word or verse that said evil man, evildoers, wicked, adulterer, liar, hypocrite, counterfeit, etc. made me think of him. I may have been wrong for feeling that way, but these scriptures brought me comfort and peace, as if the Lord was on my side. From what I was hearing, the Lord was displeased with Tory's behavior and would handle him for me.

Feeling comforted by the Word, I got out of the shower and listened to the entire book of Proverbs in less than two hours. I wanted to hear and read more. I opened my Bible and started taking notes, using other biblical translations and cross references for understanding. Over the next few days and before I knew it, I had read several other books in the Bible. I became focused and determined to know more of God's word. I studied and read daily, sometimes up to ten hours, stopping only to eat, manage hygiene, exercise, and pray.

I was so amazed at some of the stories and teachings I was learning that I didn't want to stop. I removed any distractions, including some visitors and phone calls, and I didn't go to work for over two weeks. This went on for months, and my family and friends thought I was falling into a depression. I confined myself to my home for over a month and designated a room for reading and studying.

I was led to do a twenty-four-hour spiritual fast with no food—only water. This was something I had never done; I didn't think I could do it because of my painful experiences of hunger headaches and migraines. Even though it was only twenty-four hours, that fast was hard for me. I had many thoughts of giving up and starting over at a later time, but I survived it and extended it for an additional thirty-six hours. I thought I was going to die. I came up with every excuse to give in. I was weak and starving, and my senses were at an all-time high.

My sense of smell and hunger were so high that the remains of a pot pie my son had thrown in the trash smelled like a charbroiled steak. When tempted, I drank lots of water to fill my belly, and I prayed. During that fast, my mind felt clearer, and I felt God's presence and a deeper connection with him. I was in an absolute peace that resonated through my entire body. I felt covered by a complete sense of security, and it was a humbling experience beyond human description.

The feeling made me want to keep studying, pleasing God, and doing what is right. I didn't understand my hunger for God's word, what was going on, or where it was taking me. All I knew was that it felt good, it felt right, and I wanted to stay there. It was as though I had encountered some sort of metamorphosis experience.

As I grew in knowledge and studying God's word, my intimate relationship with him and thirst for him grew stronger. It inspired me to keep seeking after him, desiring to obey him and serve him. I was learning how to hear and discern God's voice. I noticed sometimes he would answer my prayer almost immediately after early morning prayer. He would reveal or confirm things to me so clearly that it spooked me.

Each day was getting better. Things began to take root in my spiritual life, and inner healing was taking form. I started attending Bible study classes at church. Laticia Nicole's Speaklife prayer line became a safe haven and power source in my life throughout this transformation.

Not only was I growing in knowledge, my confidence was building as well. At times, I was overconfident, especially when I talked to my broken smile or reacted to another one of his painful, malignant stimuli. After months of no communication with him, I was feeling stronger and better, and I decided to unblock his number. He sent me a text message out of the blue, asking if he could come over and get some of his things. He had already taken almost everything, leaving just a few items like socks, old jackets, or tools he never used or didn't want anyway. I thought this was just an excuse to see me, and I was right. A couple texts later, Tory asked if we could talk. I asked what we needed to talk about, and he went on to say how much he missed me. He acknowledged his mistakes and said he had changed. He said he had gotten help. He didn't want a divorce, and he wanted to come home.

This turned into another lengthy conversation of what had transpired in our lives and marriage. I told Tory how gifted and smart he was and shared the amazing things that had happen to me over the past six months. I knew it could happen for him, too, if he could open his heart to Jesus Christ and allow the Lord to use him.

"I know you don't like who you are," I told Tory, "but you can't break loose from that narcissistic stronghold. You are seeking a need and putting pressure on people for something they are incapable of giving you." I felt bad knowing Tory was suffering mentally and needed healing, but coming over or coming back home was not an option.

We started praying together over the phone, and I sent Tory encouraging texts and affirmations, hoping a breakthrough would come. He started the love-bombing all over again, telling me he needed me and lying (prophe*lying*, as I called it) about what God had said to him. Tory delivered flowers and a love letter to my home for our third wedding anniversary. He said he wanted to go to the doctor and get another physical for me so he could come home.

As crazy as it may sound, I must admit it was tempting because I still loved him. I knew he was lying and hadn't changed, but my heart was hoping his transformation was true. I prayed for God to give me strength to overcome any temptation and remove any mountain, soul-ties, demonic spirits, stronghold, or person that was blocking me, hindering my blessing, producing toxicity, or keeping me from flourishing. I was intentional about this prayer but also a little nervous about what or who I might lose if the prayer was answered.

Not even one week after that prayer, the mask fell off again. Although Tory and I were living separately, I found out two different women, Jaliah and Meechie, who were around our kids' age, had been spending the night at Tory's place with their kids. A picture was sent to me of a woman taking a picture in his bedroom. He was picking their kids up from school like he was their dad. I told Tory he was sick and changing for the worse. How the heck was he playing daddy to these kids when he wasn't even answering calls from his own kids?

I told Tory I had contacted a lawyer and suggested he do the same so we could get the divorce process started. I was ready to be happy and move on with our lives. He was upset.

"Okay," he told me defiantly. "Your happiness will be in the mail."

Once the divorce was filed, I was determined to end this shameful pseudo-marriage. Tory requested I pay spousal support and his attorney fees, and he didn't want to split any of the property or assets we had acquired together during our marriage. Although Tory's income was three times higher than mine, he apparently didn't think the pain and suffering he caused me in our marriage was enough. He needed to squeeze out whatever life left in me during the divorce process.

At our last mediation, Tory had the nerve to ask our lawyers to ask me if I wanted to reconcile our marriage. I figured he had really lost his mind. The devil is a liar, so I said no. Later, Tory sent me a text message saying he still loved me and couldn't believe we were here. I replied simply, "I can. Must I remind you, you couldn't stop lying, cheating, and abusing me?" I continued. "You know God don't like ugly. The Bible says:

" *You shall not commit adultery.*"
(EXODUS 20:14 NIV)

" *But a man who commits adultery has no sense; whoever does so destroys himself.*"
(PROVERBS 6:32 NIV)

It was as if Tory didn't understand why we were in the process of divorce. I called him, and we had another lengthy conversation about whether to restore our marriage or proceed with divorce. He said he didn't want a divorce and wanted to reconcile.

"I didn't ask for a divorce because I don't love you or want to be married," I reassured him. "I didn't give up on you or our marriage. I'm giving you up to the Lord. This is a job beyond me that no human can fix. No matter how much I love you, see the potential in you to be great, and want to help, the longer I stay, the more I will get hurt. I need a divorce because I'm not safe with you; you're dangerous. You didn't and couldn't cover me, love me, lead me, or honor our marriage vows. You lack empathy, your lying and cheating is pathological, and you didn't comply with behavioral health counseling or seek wise counsel."

"Other marriages are worse than ours, and no matter what you say, you're not all innocent in this, Melanie," Tory said. "It's always me, and you think you're perfect. It wasn't all me. What about your wrongs? Just like it takes two to get married, it takes two to divorce. I will comply with giving you a divorce if you agree to another session of marriage counseling." It seemed as if he still wasn't getting it and I was getting angrier.

"Marriage counseling didn't and isn't going to work because marriage isn't the problem," I told him. "The problem is the *people* in the marriage. You are broken. Your brokenness broke me down and everything we had. This marriage can't be mended, and I can't heal in an environment that is constantly breaking me. What kind of man is okay with constantly hurting his wife and family over and over again when all we desired was to love you? What kind of man intentionally seeks woman after woman and has no desire to love them? Not to mention, your birthday just passed and you went on another cruise with a different woman from the last cruise I cancelled, and you are still seeing about ten other women. You need help! You are self-medicating with this continuous cycle of temporary satisfaction and indulging in the thrill of a new woman until you get bored or they figure you out. You cannot rely on people or things to make you happy. One thing I do know is that humans will fail you and hurt you, and it's not about *if* they will hurt you, but *when*.

"That's why it's important to give your issues to the Lord, become vulnerable, and get your heart right in him. He is your helper, your strength, and your joy comes from him. He is not a man that he shall lie, and he can do anything but fail. Jesus said,

> "*I am the way, and the truth and the life. No one comes to the Father except through me.*"
> (JOHN 14:6 NIV)

"From the day you and I met until we got married, you were thrilled and happy, loving me, showing me off, and speaking highly of me to others. You had this deep, infatuated, everlasting love for me. From what you said, I was your everything; God sent your soulmate. Until your life of secrecy was revealed, your mask fell off, and I wasn't reacting to your shenanigans in my normal loving and caring way toward you.

"You keep saying you love me. You don't know what real love is. You tell every woman you meet you love them, and you don't mean it. Love is more than just a word or feeling.

It's choosing to behave in loving ways. Love is the greatest gift of all, it's a fruit of the Holy Spirit, and you don't have that gift at all. You're good at faking it! You can be the most handsome, wealthiest man alive; you can know God's word, have all knowledge and faith that could move mountains; but if you don't have love, then you have nothing!

"As your wife, I wanted nothing more than to love you, help you, and see us through this, but no one can help you if you're not helping yourself. Until you fix your mind and heart and heal properly, you're going to continue hurting yourself, me, and others. It hurts because I love you with all my heart. I married you with good intentions of being a loving, respectful, and faithful wife, but you just completely ruined everything. I love myself more and will no longer be a victim of your abuse. This is my exodus!"

I went further, quoting scripture as a sword to hurt him and cut deeper. I told Tory there are six things the Lord hates,

" *Seven are an abomination unto him: A proud look, a lying tongue, and hands that shed innocent blood, An heart that deviseth wicked imaginations, feet that be swift in running to mischief, A false witness that speatheth lies, and he that soweth discord among brethren."*

(PROVERBS 6:16–19 KJV)

"It sounds like you are an abomination unto the Lord, since you've mastered every last one of those things," I said. "And let's not forget how you hide behind the so-called title of minister, going around praying and quoting scriptures. In reality, you are probably sicker and more in need of prayers than the people who call on you for prayer. They call on you because you call yourself a minister and know scripture. The devil knows scripture, too. You are preying on the weak and using the Word as power for your own selfish gain. God doesn't hear the prayers of evil people like you."

"*The Lord is far from the wicked, but he hears the prayers of the righteous.*"
(PROVERBS 15:29 NIV)

"*For we know that God does not listen to sinners. He listens to the godly person who does his will.*"
(JOHN 9:31 NIV)

I told Tory I felt we were definitely in our last days because second Timothy chapter three spoke about these terrible times and people like him:

" *lovers of themselves, lovers of money, boastful, proud, abusive, disobedient to their parents, ungrateful, unholy, without love, unforgiving, slanderous, without self-control, brutal, not lovers of the good, treacherous, rash, conceited, lovers of pleasure rather than lovers of God, having a form of godliness but denying its power. Have nothing to do with such people."*

(2 TIMOTHY 3:2–5 NIV)

"This scripture right here should have your picture next to it," I told Tory.

"*They are the kind who worm their way into homes and gain control over gullible women, who are loaded down with sins and are swayed by all kinds of evil desires, always learning but never able to come to a knowledge of the truth."*

(2 TIMOTHY 3:6–7 NIV)

"*But they will not get very far because, as in the case of those men, their folly will be clear to everyone."*

(2 TIMOTHY 3:9 NIV)

I brought up a verse that made me think of Tory's frequent nightmares and night terrors that would make him jump up out of his sleep screaming, shaking, and trembling in terror.

"Why do you think you have those night terrors?" I asked. "Because your spirit is wicked and can't rest. There is no peace for the wicked. You live a life of secrecy and darkness."

"For they cannot rest until they do evil; they are robbed of sleep till they make someone stumble. They eat the bread of wickedness and drink the wine of violence."

(PROVERBS 4:16–17 NIV)

"You're always saying you need me and I'm all you have when that's not true. You have four gifted, beautiful, very intelligent kids that need you, and you need them. Those kids need their father, but you're too busy running behind all these different women, playing victim and acting like you don't have any family. You have failed at least three marriages doing the same thing, and you failed getting help. *You* may be the reason you claim to have no one and are losing people."

Yes, I said all those mean, hurtful things to him. It felt good giving him a dose of his own pain back, using scripture to prove how bad a person he was, and telling him the Lord was not going to let him get away with hurting me.

Tory replied, "You're acting as if you're so perfect, but you're not; no one is. God's mercy is bountiful. The same grace and mercy he gives you is available to me. Do not grow weary in doing good, Melanie. Don't treat me like I treated you. Truth without love is still brutality. Melanie, you are a powerful woman, and I never allowed anyone to get close to me as I allowed you. You are different and have the power to build me up, make me feel like I'm superman and can fly. But lately, you've been good at making me feel like I'm worthless. You may be right: I do need help breaking soul-ties, generational cures, and spirits that may be on me. I need you to help fast and pray for me to break the strongholds you think are on me.

"I saw on the news that a man committed suicide after reading thousands of negative texts from his girlfriend. That's how you've been making me feel lately. I admit, I've hurt you and done a lot of things wrong. I didn't do you right, I hurt a lot of people, and I know I need help. I'm sorry; I hope to get it right one day, but verbally abusing me and quoting Bible verses at me is not going to help me or change me. I know scripture, too.

"On judgment day," Tory continued, "God isn't going to judge you based on what I did; you're going to be judged on what *you* did. One day, I hope you can find it in your heart to forgive me. I see you have been studying more of God's word. I remember that I was once where you are when I needed to get closer to the Lord. Whatever you are doing in Christ, please don't stop, and please don't stop praying for me."

His response was a triple hitter. It bruised my ego, touched my soul, and provoked an awakening and awareness inside of me. Tory was right: what I was doing to him was wrong. Even though I didn't want to hear it, I needed to. I was judging him.

" *D* o not judge, or you too will be judged. For the same way you judge others, you will be judged, and with the measure you use, it will be measured to you."

(MATTHEW 7:1–2 NIV).

" *There is only one Lawgiver and Judge, the one who is able to save and destroy. But you- who are you to judge your neighbor?"*

(JAMES 4:12 NIV)

" *Out of the same mouth come praise and cursing. My brothers and sisters, this should not be."*

(JAMES 3:10 KJV)

In anger I said some mean and hurtful things to him. I was hurting and lashing back with my words. I needed to own my wrongs in this. Sometimes it's not the physical blows that hurt most; the words coming out of our mouths can cause the worst pain and damage. Our words are powerful and can't be erased.

The Bible says

" *Death and life are in the power of the tongue; and they that love it shall eat the fruit thereof."*

(PROVERBS 18:21 KJV)

The words we speak will either build us up or tear us down. The book of James tells us

" *And among all the parts of the body, the tongue is a flame of fire. It is a whole world of wickedness, corrupting your entire body. It can set your whole life on fire, for it is set on fire by hell itself."*

(JAMES 3:6 NLT)

"Get rid of all bitterness, rage and anger, brawling and slander, along with every form of malice. Be kind and compassionate to one another, forgiving each other, just as in Christ God forgave you."

(EPHESIANS 4:31–32 NIV)

My anger toward Tory let me know I hadn't truly forgiven him and had not completely healed. I wanted and needed to truly forgive Tory and grow in that area. I had gained knowledge, insight, and inspiration, but I was still harboring bitterness and brokenness. I needed a deep self-assessment. I had more work and growing to do in Christ.

I had never intended to use God's word to hurt or abuse others, or to fight low-level conflicts with it. Since I've encountered God's merciful, gracious splendor on so many different levels, I was intentional about being spiritually aligned. I wanted to authentically heal, cultivate self-awareness, identify myself in God, view myself as God does, and be conscious of how God wanted to use me.

I stopped praying for God to change Tory and began asking God to change me. I began to pray and ask God for those character-building traits that would allow my character to reflect Him. I wanted to create a greater atmosphere of forgiveness, peace, love, and healing from within. Therefore, it was necessary that I relied on Him for direction as I embarked on this new journey. I started dating myself, reducing distractions, reading more, and engaging in spiritually empowering groups and conferences. I started visiting my childhood family church and rejoined.

No one should go through their brokenness alone. It is important to be around people who are positive influences. I thank God for placing some amazing people in my life, from family and friends to even my frenemies. I'm thankful for them all, for they either blessed me or helped push me toward my purpose. God blessed me with a praying mother, dad, kids, siblings, family, Teresa Moore, and other sisters in Christ to stand in the gap, interceding on my behalf and adopting my burdens in prayer.

I'm thankful for my aunt, Evangelist Cross, who consistently helped plant the word of God within me and shared the importance of forgiving Tory. Countless blessings came from a decision to join a travel company in 2017. I joined under marketing director Laticia Nicole, who was also a sister in Christ and business partner. Laticia Nicole is a registered nurse, philanthropist, entrepreneur, author, minister, mentor, coach, and founder of Speaklife ministry. Along with my aunt, Laticia became one of my spiritual mentors by speaking life, pouring and planting positive seeds of affirmations, motivation, and inspiration within me, all rooted in the word of God.

They emphasized the importance of having a strong spiritual foundation. It is key and essential for building relationships, businesses, or ministry, and it starts within us. To bring forth success, we must apply those kingdom principles to every area of our lives. Throughout the process, I wanted to keep my life private. I was often nervous, fearful, and uncomfortable. I learned that healing and success don't happen in comfort zones.

I may not be where I want to be, but I'm so thankful I'm not where I used to be. I'm thankful for every day I wake up. I praise God and try to be a better person than I was yesterday. I'm not denying reality; I'm still a work in progress. There are areas in my life where I am in recovery. I'm not perfect and never will be, but I will make an effort to grow in Christ daily. I know life isn't always easy. I will be tempted daily. I will hurt someone. I will get hurt, afflicted, and tried as long as I'm alive. But God's word showed me that if I keep my faith in him, stay connected to him, and put on the whole armor of God, he will help me. He will deliver me, he will protect me, he will forgive me, and he will help me to forgive. Even in the midst of this coronavirus pandemic, racial inequity, and uncertain times, I trust God with my tomorrow because he was faithful with my yesterday.

"*Never will I leave you: never will I forsake you.*"
(HEBREWS 13:5 NIV)

"*No temptation has overtaken you except what is common to mankind. And God is faithful: he will not let you be tempted beyond what you can bear. But when you are tempted, he will also provide a way out so that you can endure it.*"
(1 CORINTHIANS 10:13 NIV)

"*The Lord is good, a strong refuge when trouble comes. He is close to those who trust in him.*"

(NAHUM 1:7 NLT).

God showed up at a time in my life when I had lost all hope. I was in a dark place and couldn't see any light. He showed up when I was so broken that I didn't think a shattered piece of glass like me was fixable. He made sure I knew it was his saving grace that brought me out of the spiritual infirmities.

God knew all along about Tory. He knew the broken smile was the perfect way to break my smile, so he could smile through me. I now see that I was *Beautifully Broken.*

I believe *Beautifully Broken* was God's way of rebuilding my broken soul with his love, grace, knowledge, elegance, and mindfulness. I am embracing it as a part of my testimony, giving God all the praise and glory!

Revelation 12:11 KJV says,

"*And they overcame him by the blood of the lamb, and by the word of their testimony; and they loved not their lives unto the death.*"

the author's closing words

Heartache Versus Heartbroken (Brokenness)

We all can agree brokenness hurts, no doubt. In my years of dating, I had never actually experienced a real heartbreak. Yes, I had been hurt many times and suffered heartache, but the pain didn't persist, and I was able to move on with minimal effects.

A heartache to me is short-lived, occurring with some emotional stress and feelings, something like a stubbed toe or paper cut. But a broken heart is a whole other world of overwhelming emotional, mental, physical stress and seemingly never-ending excruciating pain—suffering felt in your heart, spirit, and flesh.

A broken heart can take many forms: depression, anxiety, guilt, suicidal/homicidal ideations, bitterness, shame, addiction, and unhealthy behavior patterns. If dismissed or not properly healed, a broken heart can end up deceiving us and making things worse. There are people clinically treating brokenness that need spiritual healing, and there are some who need both. Some people don't want to change because they receive too much attention and sympathy by staying broken. That's why it is important to get to the root of our brokenness and properly heal, emotionally, mentally, physically, and spiritually.

Before I learned I was spiritually broken, I didn't know I was broken. I didn't *feel* broken. I thought I was good. Spiritual depression is one of the reasons I carried feelings of incompleteness and emptiness throughout the years. The solution to emptiness is fulfillment, a thirst only God could fulfill.

My brokenness wouldn't allow me to face the red flags that were present prior to my marriage. My brokenness was a doorway for the adversary to present himself as a Godsend, my knight in shining armor, masking his demons and brokenness.

Some people would think being a teenage mother of two kids in high school and raising them alone would be my greatest trial to overcome. It was hard, but it wasn't the greatest. My greatest trial was being married to a narcissist and coming out in my right mind safe and alive.

The traumatic effects of my husband's narcissistic personality, serial malignant infidelity, and betrayal played a significant part in my breakdown. I had to face my grief and wrestle with all stages of it. But God's presence gave me strength and courage to walk through that dark valley that felt like death.

" *The Lord is close to the brokenhearted and saves those who are crushed in spirit.*"

(PSALMS 34:18 NIV)

In the process of my brokenness, I have learned that God sometimes uses our brokenness for his glory. Although the world may despise broken people, God takes pleasure in using broken things. In fact, God demands we be broken before he can begin to use us. Broken makes us useful to God and can bring us close to him.

I now see the value in brokenness because there are some things God can only do in us when we are broken. When we are broken, depleted, and drained with nothing left to give, we realize we can't do it on our own. When the only way out is *through,* we are more open and willing to hear from God. He uses those moments to reveal our issues to us so we can see ourselves as he sees us.

Our brokenness, suffering, and trials are never wasted. God uses them to deepen our understanding in a few different ways.

For him: He wants us to get to know him, grow closer to him, trust and have faith in him.

For us: Brokenness helps develop us in certain areas of our lives, building character and helping us understand who we are and to be made whole.

For others: Our brokenness helps others increase their growth in Christ. Other people's brokenness offers an opportunity to love and understand through their brokenness, and help give others hope in Christ through our struggles.

"*The sacrifices of God are a broken spirit: A broken and a contrite heart—These, O God, You will not despise.*"

(PSALM 51:17 NKJV)

Just like God used me and has saved many other broken people, he can use anyone, including you and my broken smile. God can create a radical transformation.

1 Corinthians 2:9 lets us know God is able to do "what no eye has seen, what no ear has heard, and what not human mind has conceived." These are the things God has prepared for those who love him. Philippians 4:13 says, "I can do all things through Christ who strengthens me."

God can do powerful things in our lives. He can do anything but fail.

And without faith, it is impossible to please God, because anyone who comes to him must believe that he exists and he rewards those who earnestly seek him (Hebrews 11:6).

The Power and Importance of Forgiveness

"*And when you stand praying, if you hold anything against anyone, forgive them, so that your Father in heaven may forgive your sin. But if you do not forgive, neither will your Father in heaven forgive your sins.*"

(MARK 11:25-26 NIV)

My experience with brokenness has helped me understand that forgiving someone who hurt you is not always easy. It can be a difficult process because forgiveness isn't natural, it's spiritual. It took me some time to grasp the process of forgiveness and forgive my broken smile, but with the help of God, I was able to forgive him.

It's not the end of the world if someone hurt you, rejected you, cheated on you, or didn't love you. Most of us think it's the enemy that comes and interrupts our so-called happy lives, when it could very well be God's divine intervention. Some things come into our lives like a wrecking ball because some renovation requires demolition. God doesn't want us to settle for less than we deserve; therefore, he must intervene to move us into our new season. How can you prepare for the person God has for you if you are still holding on to someone who has hurt you, doesn't deserve you, keeps you in bondage, or is no longer a part of your purpose? I forgave Tory and asked for his forgiveness. I wished him well and continue to pray for his well-being.

According to the American Psychological Association, forgiveness is the intentional and conscious decision to release feelings of resentment, bitterness, revenge, or negative emotions toward someone who has hurt you, whether or not they deserve your forgiveness or feel sorry for what they did to you. Forgiveness is not excusing or forgetting that someone wronged you. It doesn't mean you are completely healed or free of the effects, and it doesn't mean you have to reconcile with the person, either. Forgiving someone you don't want to forgive is being obedient to God, and that is what breaks the enemy's power. Forgiveness is a gift from you to yourself! Holding on to grudges and resentment is a lot of work and keeps you from living a life of happiness.

Resentment and toxic emotions are known to activate diseases in our bodies and minds. Forgiveness creates healing from the mental stress and emotional bondage that keep you from living your best life. Forgiveness liberates the soul and gives life. We can't change our yesterday, but we all can change our tomorrow.

Mistakes, failures, flaws, and guilt are a part of being human, and it's okay to feel guilty. Guilt can serve a purpose because with guilt, you understand what you did wrong and how you can repair the situation, which can motivate us to correct our wrongs. *We have to forgive ourselves.* Self-forgiveness is just as important as forgiving others. Sometimes it can be harder to forgive ourselves than it is to forgive those who hurt us. Self-forgiving involves facing past failures, confessing what we did wrong, and taking ownership of our wrongs. Self-forgiveness is letting go of what we are holding against ourselves so we can move on and receive the fullness of God's plan and blessings for our lives.

Forgiveness is a part of spiritual maturity and is necessary for us to clean our hearts of resentment, anger, bitterness or other emotions that block us from being used by God. When we align our thoughts and hearts with God's will for forgiveness, that's when miraculous healing begins. Hurt people hurt other people, but healed people can heal others.

"*Forget the former things; do not dwell on the past. See, I am doing a new thing! Now it springs up; do you not perceive it? I am making a way in the wilderness and streams in the wasteland.*"

(ISAIAH 43:18–19 NIV)

acknowledgements

irst and foremost, praises and thanks to God, the
Almighty, the Author and Finisher of my life, for his
many blessings and the accomplishment of this book. I
never could have done this without his strength, knowledge,
grace, and patience. Lord, I thank you for the courage and
strength to bring forth the manifestation of this book. Thank
you for the heart to serve you and your people.

To my mother, Pearlene Talbert, thank you for being my
number one cheerleader and supporter. Thank you for the
countless times you've been there for me, encouraging me,
guiding me, and praying for me when I needed it the most.
For loving me unconditionally as I journey through this
thing called life. Thank you for all you do and all that you
are and adding love to everything you do. I'm so blessed to
have a mother like you.

Rest in paradise to my stepfather, Keith Talbert, who
helped raise me since I was a toddler. To my dad, Michael
Nolan, and stepmother, Joann, thank you for your love,

being there to lend an ear or share your wisdom. To my kids, Cheyna Walker and Ajanee McGraw, although we grew up together, thank you for your love and being patient with me when I wasn't patient with you. You both have motivated, encouraged, and been more than a blessing to me. You gave me strength to keep pushing and trusting God. To my grandson, Aiden Armstead, I love my honey. You bring me so much joy. To my grandson's father, Darryl (Malik) Armstead, thank you for always being there for Boogie, no matter the time, day or night.

To my sister, Chef Kimberly Johnson, my right leg, thank you for your unlimited selfless acts of kindness, generosity, and unconditional love. You are the epitome of the best sister anyone could have. To my brothers, Michael McGraw and Keith Talbert Jr., thank you for your unconditional love, support, and always having my back. You guys are the truth. My cousin Juanita Johnson, thank you for always being there and taking me under your wing as your little sister since I was a little girl.

To Teresa Moore, my sister in Christ, you are the epitome of a true friend, mother, wife, daughter, and sister. I've been blessed to have you as my friend for over twenty years. Thank you for your support, love, and for being my prayer partner and always telling me the truth, even when I don't want to hear it. Thank you for adopting my burdens and your intercession on my behalf in prayer. To Rebecca Robinson, thank you for over twenty years of being a true friend and supporter. No matter how far away you are, night or day, you're always there for me. To Evangelist Laticia Nicole

Beatty and Speaklife Prayer Ministry, thank you for the many blessings you sowed into my life and your inspiration throughout this journey. Without you, this vision would not have come to pass. To my aunt Evangelist Juanita Cross, thank you for your love, guidance, and prayers. Thank you for planting the word of God into my life and believing in me. Love you, continue resting in paradise.

Special Thanks to Monique D. Mensah and Make Your Mark Publishing Solutions. Thank you to everyone who has been there, supported, or pushed me to greater heights. I have been blessed to have so many amazing people in my life. There are too many to name. To all my nieces, nephews, my godson, aunties, uncles, grandparents, family, friends, coworkers, and business partners, Victoria Cregett, Sonya Scott, Tracy Pickett, Rose Keglar, Fayego Jefferson, Dakima Hicks, LaSonja Cade, and Thomas Walker, you have my sincerest thanks.

Covid19 Frontliners

A special thanks and gratitude for all the healthcare and essential workers. Sinai Grace Emergency Department has some of the toughest, hardworking, compassionate, strongest, persevering, heroes, sheroes, and dedicated nurses. No one will ever know our stories unless they've worked in our shoes. You guys rock!

My prayers and heartfelt condolences for all whose lives have been touched by this tragedy. For those who mourn the loss of a loved one, I pray the Lord comforts, heals, and fills your void with his presence.

notes from loved ones

To my daughter Melanie,

From the day you were born, I knew you were going to be someone special. You are honestly one of the most motivated, consistent, determined people I know, so strong and beautiful inside and out. I knew you would accomplish all your dreams. I hope your book sells millions, and I know it will truly be a blessing to those who read it. May God continue to bless you in all your endeavors.

Love you sincerely,
Mom

From your daughter Cheyna,

Mom, I just want to take the time out to tell you how proud I am of you. You are such a motivational and inspiring woman. You go for what you want, and you don't stop until you get what you want. Looking at you grow into the woman you are today, I couldn't be happier. We grew up together. You raised two beautiful kids all on your own, worked three jobs, and did whatever you had to do to make sure your kids were safe and our needs were met. I applaud you so much. You're the best mom a daughter can ask for. You are the hardest working woman I know, and you don't stop until you accomplish your goals. I am so happy to call you my mother. You are a PHENOMENAL WOMAN! Continue to be blessed, prosper, and walk into your purpose God wants you to walk in. I love you with everything in me, Mom, so much. Congratulations on your first book. You actually did what you said you were going to do, and for that, I'm excited to see what the future brings you. You are the true definition of what dedication and determination is.

Love you always,
Your baby girl, Cheyna

Thank you for reading *My Broken Smiles Beautifully Broken*

If you enjoyed this book, please leave an online review.

KEEP IN TOUCH WITH MELANIE SMILES

Website: www.melaniesmiles.com
Facebook: Melanie Smiles
Instagram: @ mel_rnsmiles
Email: info@melaniesmiles.com

CPSIA information can be obtained
at www.ICGtesting.com
Printed in the USA
LVHW040059140920
665919LV00001B/58